Preaching the Blues

Preaching the Blues: Black Feminist Performance in Lynching Plays examines several lynching plays to foreground black women's performances as non-normative subjects who challenge white supremacist ideology.

Maisha S. Akbar re-maps the study of lynching drama by examining plays that are contingent upon race-based settings in black households versus white households. She also discusses performances of lynching plays at Historically Black Colleges and Universities (HBCUs) in the South and reviews lynching plays closely tied to black school campuses. By focusing on current examples and impacts of lynching plays in the public sphere, this book grounds this historical form of theatre in the present day with depth and relevance.

Of interest to scholars and students of both general Theatre and Performance Studies, and of African American Theatre and Drama, *Preaching the Blues* foregrounds the importance of black feminist artists in lynching culture and interdisciplinary scholarship.

Maisha S. Akbar is Associate Professor of Theatre and Performance Studies at Fort Valley State University, where she is founding coordinator of a Theatre and Performance Studies academic curriculum. Dr. Akbar's research interests include black feminist performance studies and psychoanalysis. More information on her work can be found at www.blackplaybook.com.

Preaching the Blues

Black Feminist Performance in Lynching Plays

Maisha S. Akbar

Taylor & Francis Group

LONDON AND NEW YORK

First published 2020
by Routledge
2 Park Square, Milton Park, Abingdon, Oxon OX14 4RN

and by Routledge
605 Third Avenue, New York, NY 10017

First issued in paperback 2021

Routledge is an imprint of the Taylor & Francis Group, an informa
business

Publisher's Note
The publisher has gone to great lengths to ensure the quality of this
reprint but points out that some imperfections in the original copies
may be apparent.

British Library Cataloguing-in-Publication Data
A catalogue record for this book is available from the British
Library

Library of Congress Cataloging-in-Publication Data
A catalog record for this book has been requested

ISBN 13: 978-1-03-208849-5 (pbk)
ISBN 13: 978-1-138-47961-6 (hbk)

Typeset in Garamond
by Apex CoVantage, LLC

For my children, Khalil Akbar and Mecca Akbar;
my parents, Na'im Shabazz and Beverly Kilbourne; and
my grandparents, Charles and Clarina Williams and David
and Mary Blevins.

I also dedicate this work to Stacey Abrams for her
strength, courage and refusal to concede.

Contents

Acknowledgments

All Praise is due to Allah.

This project culminates as a "life's work," which entails a lifetime's worth of acknowledgments.

Many thanks to my colleagues at Fort Valley State University with whom I've collaborated and who have supported my dramatic and academic productions. Rickey Calloway, Elizabeth Hamilton and Justice Yorke prove invaluable for their creative collaboration, support and encouragement. I am also grateful to Bobby Dickey and Andrew Lee for their continued support, as well as to Brigitte Hall for her friendship. I owe Frank Mahitab, James Scott and Betty Rogers special thanks for all of their courtesy in helping me access library references. I will always treasure Uppinder Mehan's example, guidance and feedback in helping me develop this project through its middle, yet still awkward stage. I will always be inspired by the genius of Franklin Gross and Ya-Hui Cheng.

Foremost on my list of appreciation goes to my Fort Valley State University drama students with whom creative collaboration has been rewarding and exhilarating. Thank you, Renee Bynum, Kenny Bowman, Josean Pittman, Dana Jefferson, Amanda Allen, Kadeem Ambrose, Kierra Bennett, Anna Fuller, Jeff Pierre, Ashley Williams, Britni Moore, Marquita Garnes, Matthew Brown, Foster Ford, Laniah Smith, Jewayne Coffee, Shanice Bates, Jaukeem Balcom, Karli Brown, A.J. Browning, Mikkira Bullard, Alexandra Neal, Tiara Harry, Stephanie McNeil, Kebriana Ross, Delicia James Katherine Bakrania, Christopher Millican and Ebony White.

I am in awe of the generosity, example and mentorship of Kathy A. Perkins and Judith L. Stephens. Your support and encouragement of this work as well as my career endeavors means the world to me.

I am grateful many times over to have Barry Brummett in my life as extended family, mentor and friend. Thank you so much for being the special person that you are.

I think and speak so often about my earliest mentors who set me on my path as a cultural scholar that you wouldn't know that they've been gone from my life for 30 years and 15 years respectively. The wisdom of Dr. L.L. Haynes Jr. and Alan Dundes will forever be part of my life, and I will be forever grateful to them as my donor figures on my life's journey.

Nikol Alexander-Floyd gets the recognition as a peer scholar by whom I've been inspired since we were undergraduates at Southern University and A&M College many moons ago. It's been all these years and you're still leading by example. Thank you for being the first scholar that I sat next to in class whom I could look up to. You've never ceased to be an amazing example and colleague. We, as Scrappy Scribblers, must begin a tally of our project output!

Personally, I appreciate Joel Bryant for his love, friendship and understanding of me as an artist and producer.

Peace and love to my family whom I try to represent to the fullest.

Introduction

On February 14, 2019, after more than 100 years and nearly 200 attempts, the United States Senate passed anti-lynching legislation, the Justice for Victims of Lynching Act. Championed by senators Kamala Harris (D-California), Cory Booker (D-New Jersey) and Tim Scott (R-South Carolina), the bill not only reflects a culmination of efforts by United States legislators, but those first spearheaded in 1892 by Ida B. Wells-Barnett (1862–1931), a black woman anti-lynching/rape activist, journalist and critical cultural scholar. Through Wells-Barnett's weekly newspaper, *Free Speech*, as well as in her pamphlets, including *Southern Horrors: Lynch Law in All Its Phases* (1892), *A Red Record* (1895) and *Mob Rule in New Orleans* (1900), Wells-Barnett initiated an anti-lynching movement protesting lynching as white supremacist discursive and material performance that would serve as a foundation for all other anti-lynching efforts. Such campaigns include those implemented by the National Association for the Advancement of Colored People (NAACP), the Association of Southern Women for the Prevention of Lynching (ASWPL) as well as proposals of early anti-lynching legislation such as the Dyer Bill (1918) and the Costigan-Wagner Act (1934).

Despite its overwhelming significance as black feminist cultural production igniting cross-generational, interracial anti-lynching movement(s), Wells-Barnett's activism, which is noted by biographer Patricia A. Schechter to be made up of "protest activity and community building," was subject to concealment "within the discourses and practices of female reform and black politics in the United States."[1] Ida B. Wells-Barnett's anti-lynching/rape activism could not escape subjugation to "feminization," and/or race and class-based marginalization despite the groundbreaking nature of her efforts.[2] Wells-Barnett's black feminist cultural production constituted a first wave of protest against lynching performances as white supremacist ideology *par excellence*, but not the last, to be obscured by racist and sexist political mechanizations. In much the same way as Wells-Barnett's investigational journalism, speechmaking and public protest, anti-lynching plays were also subject to obscurity as a genre of American theatre. Anti-lynching plays, defined by Judith L. Stephens as "a play in which the threat or occurrence of a lynching, past or present, has a major impact on the dramatic action," comprise a "distinct genre of American drama," functioning as both "a dramatic record of racial history in the United States and a continuously evolving dramatic form that preserves the knowledge of this particular form of racial violence and the memory of its victims."[3] Lynching plays extended upon Wells-Barnett's activism (as well as anti-lynching campaigns of other prominent organizations) by using theatre as a public mode of communication by which to challenge lynching as whiteness performance even while setting the plays within private or secret domains.

Black women's political and artistic challenges to lynching reflect their view of the practice as whiteness cultural performance despite efforts to characterize it otherwise. Since performance constitutes "an essentially contested concept,"[4] (anti-) lynching playwrights used theatre to contest lynching as white supremacist ideology thereby reconciling "aesthetic versus political" as well as a "public versus private" binaries implicit within Western metaphysics. In short, the anti-lynching play genre constitutes an explicitly performance-based anti-lynching movement spearheaded by black women, yet creating for black and white women playwrights alike, a common ideological and aesthetic ground.[5] As artist-activists, lynching playwrights did not necessarily expect "to defeat or silence opposing positions, but rather through continuing dialogue to attain a sharper articulation of all positions and therefore a fuller understanding of the conceptual richness of performance."[6] Lynching playwrights effectively used lynching plays as a space in which a mediation of post-Reconstruction politics could take place, an endeavor Reconstruction's failure left incomplete. Lynching plays are found to undertake a remapping of cognitive and aesthetic categories, not only disputing performative constructions of race and gender, but also engaging in critical examinations of time and "place," especially with regard to social order as well as Jim Crow segregation.

Preaching the Blues examines anti-lynching plays as a black feminist performance tradition comprised of specific (counterhegemonic) communicative strategies and practices opposing lynching as white supremacist performance. Lynching plays function as intercultural repositories of respective black and white performance traditions, although the genre was subject to oppression, misrecognition and doubt as black feminist cultural production. In order to conduct such close readings, *Preaching the Blues* examines lynching plays using performance theory and/or a performative lens as a paradigmatic framework through which to understand its revisionist practices, a heretofore underemphasized undertaking. When viewed as "repetition of disempowered acts,"[7] lynching plays (as a genre) can be read for both its black feminist ideological constructions as well as its aesthetic conventions. Both anti-lynching dramatists as well as the black women subjects within lynching plays can be understood to perform "a special class of actions that are derived from and may be plotted within a grid of power relations"[8] (i.e. white supremacy) thereby making possible richer analysis of black feminist performance strategies performed in and around the plays, including those practiced by Ida B. Wells-Barnett and other anti-lynching activists both preceding and following the anti-lynching play movement, such as Mary Church Terrell's 1904 essay, "Lynching from a Negro's Point of View," Mary B. Talbert's Anti-Lynching Crusade in 1922, and Mary McLeod Bethune's 1930 statement urging southern white women to assume responsibility for halting the rise in racial violence.[9]

Analyzing lynching plays through a performance studies-based framework foregrounds the genre as early interdisciplinary cultural studies through which lynching playwrights reframed lynching performances as whiteness social drama to create a novel theatre genre.[10] At the same time, lynching plays are found to undermine "the coherence of categories like the personal and political by seeing individual acts as inseparable from complex discursive power relations"[11] thereby collectivizing black feminist performance strategies, whether used by social and political activists, literary artists, clubwomen,[12] imprisoned women, musicians, dancers, visual artists or lynching playwrights. When challenging white supremacist performance practices, black feminisms can now be recognized as part of a corresponding cross-generational and/or multi-disciplinary tradition.

A particularly cogent example that can be tied to both lynching playwrights' remapping of lynching performances as well as recent anti-lynching legislation efforts is evidenced in an exchange between New Negro era literary artist Georgia Douglas Johnson (1877?–1966), the genre's most prolific playwright,[13] and Walter White, executive secretary of the NAACP. Johnson first documented an ongoing legislative struggle to outlaw lynching in anti-lynching plays she wrote; however, she faced discrimination in getting them produced, reflecting the same denial of institutional access faced by Wells-Barnett.[14] According to Johnson biographer and anti-lynching play scholar Judith L. Stephens' *The Plays of Georgia Douglass Johnson* (2006), Johnson presented her lynching plays to the NAACP for possible production by its Youth Council, only to have White return the plays due to their depictions of negative outcomes to which he referred as "ending in defeat." Despite Johnson's attempt to explain to White her expert reasoning for including a less than ideal ending without compromising the plays' "greatest dramatic moments," the organization never produced her submitted work. Later, as part of a 1938 anti-lynching campaign, the NAACP summoned Johnson to write a short lynching play which resulted in *And Yet They Paused* (1938) and *A Bill to Be Passed* (1938), two very similar one-act plays with different endings.[15] Both plays represent the events surrounding a 1936 lynching in Duck Hill, Mississippi, in which two black men were tied to trees and burned with flame throwers at the exact same moment Congress considered anti-lynching legislation as presented by Joseph Gavagan (D-New York). Johnson's plays depict Congressional activity, especially filibustering or "stallin'," as whiteness performance preventing passage of the legislation. When contrasted, *A Bill to Be Passed* ends on a positive note – the bill passes the House, while *And Yet They Paused* ends in "defeat" with regard to both the legislation as well an active lynching taking place. Despite White's earlier criticism of her dramatic images, Johnson maintained a steadfastness in presenting a less than positive outcome in *And Yet They Paused*, instead choosing to accurately represent a failed Congressional attempt to pass anti-lynching legislation. Johnson did not back down from her position but instead presented two versions of the drama, including an addendum on *A Bill to Be Passed* that facilitated other statements the organization wanted to make about legislative efforts.[16] Not only did Johnson maintain her "artistic integrity as a playwright and her dedication to her own vision of theatre as social protest,"[17] her illumination of the circumstances surrounding Congress' inability to pass anti-lynching legislation has stood the test of time, even until the present day.

A close reading of Johnson's anti-lynching play *And Yet They Paused* accurately represents one of Congress' 200 failed attempts to pass anti-lynching legislation as a one-act play in four scenes. Interestingly, Johnson juxtaposes traditional black church performance or "ring shout" performance,[18] with whiteness performance as practiced by white Congressmen. In a point to which I will return, black Mississippi church members sing "Walls of Jericho" and "Go Down Moses" while they await news about Congress' proceedings on anti-lynching legislation from a church elder (Jasper Greene) and delegate (Williams) who have been sent to Washington as community representatives. Interposed with their spirituals and prayers is news of the local lynching of a black citizen which occurs concurrently.

In the fourth and final scene, church delegate Williams and Elder Jasper Greene stand outside the doors of Congress which they cannot enter while a reporter listens and interprets the session proceedings to them. Upon hearing of Congressional stalling and then breaking for recess, the reporter explains: "Just the same handful of crackers holding out so's the bill can't be passed. They know what side their bread is buttered on. They want to come back to Congress – they know what they're doing!" Here, Johnson indicates that Congress avoids passing the bill in order to get re-elected rather than doing the right thing in a moral sense. "It's a sin and a shame" cites the reporter to which Williams extorts: "They don't want to finish. They want to keep us on the cross." When the Congress returns to a late night session, they receive a telegraph with the news of the latest lynching victim in Mississippi. The play ends with a call to action as one of the Congressmen urges the others to pass the bill.

Similarly, *A Bill to Be Passed* is written in the same four-scene structure as *And Yet They Paused*, each scene depicting a different time of day. In the final night scene, however, Johnson depicts a fuller debate among the Congressmen who upon receiving news of the Mississippi lynching are moved to act beyond filibustering to actually consider the legislation. The Congressmen's arguments, as conveyed by the reporter, reflect positions that Williams and Elder Jasper Greene identify as (whiteness, rhetorical) "smokescreens" or just plain, "crazy." Such rebuttals include arguments claiming that the bill's true intention is to "break the spirit of the white South" by fostering "social equality" or mongrelizing whites[19] as well as the bill's encouragement of blacks "to commit rape." However, upon an appeal to vote upon their consciences instead of in response to lynching as a racial problem, the Congressmen take a vote and the bill passes the House.

Finally, as aforementioned, Johnson compares black performance practices to white ones by juxtaposing the black church to a white Congress. Black anti-lynching activists are represented as church members who, in their struggle for justice, invoke Biblical images such as Joshua and the Battle of Jericho, Moses versus Pharaoh and Daniel in the Lion's Den. Not only are these archetypes relevant to black citizens' everyday struggle for justice in the fight against lynching, they also echo "ring shout" songs as first performed in secret and then sung by black Christians when converting to Christianity during the Great Awakening.[20] The ring shout is best known for the counter-clockwise direction in which performers moved, its polyrhythmic hand clapping and foot stomping as well as a call and response vocal patterning. Johnson's inclusion of these specific songs indicates black Christians' interpretation of the religious tradition in a way that served them and mitigated the challenges they endured.

Using a ring shout performance framework, Johnson effectively ritualized her lynching plays into a dramatic form to which black audience members could connect and participate. Johnson thereby employs an influential and transformative power of theatre to affect the audience. Johnson's play structure operates as call and response although the white Congressional response does not reflect empathy or respect for black humanity. Johnson uses the ring shout to effectively negotiate a reconciliation of the Western binary realms between the personal and the political, African worship practices and Christianity as well as the sacred and secular. Finally, Johnson's drama reflects an intention for her plays to be useful as praxis to the audiences in which they were produced, an approach that was so novel that her critics were unable to comprehend it.

Even further, through the call and response performance incorporated as part of representing the ring shout, Johnson's plays perform affectively for black church members who show respect for each other's humanity by addressing each other using gender-based family terms, "Brother" and "Sister," a black performance practice acknowledging a positionality as "all God's children" who deserve protection as such. To extend upon Stephens' foregrounding of the practice, I would add that the black church members' utterance of "Brother" and "Sister" as an act of *Signifying*, which according to Claudia Mitchell-Kernan, emphasizes indirection and refers to "a particular kind of language specialization" that "defines the black community as a speech community in contrast to non-Black communities."[21] Unlike other communities in which hierarchical differences are emphasized, use of the monikers "Brother" and "Sister" in the black church establishes an ideal black familial relationship among siblings in which everyone is seen as equal to each other. The relationship among fellow black church members can be understood as an alternative to patriarchy, as radically democratic, loving and just.

The white Congress, on the other hand, is presented in Johnson's plays as a sphere of abuse of power, cronyism and injustice. As aforementioned, the whiteness performance practices of filibustering, stalling, illogical argumentation and face saving explain the failure to pass anti-lynching legislation into law. The ongoing practice of lynching as executed by mobs challenges the very democracy that the Congressmen are sworn to uphold. In his way, Johnson depicts the Congressmen as secular American hypocrites who fail in their responsibilities as keepers of the United States Constitution. Even further, the active Mississippi lynching effectively mirrors the failure of Congress to enact justice by passing anti-lynching legislation.

An introduction to critical lynching studies

Traditionally, scholars examining lynching have focused on "the lynching era," or the period between 1865 and 1930, when lynching blacks . . . became *a systematic* (emphasis mine) feature of race relations" in order to examine the practice.[22] More specifically, lynching African Americans flourished in the 1880s, when "lynchings assumed an overtly racial character, with nearly 80 percent of all victims being black males."[23] Interestingly, this era does not only constitute a proverbial American crossroads with regard to race relations, but it is also identified as "a crucible of change in gender and sexual relations"[24] as well. In fact, English and women's studies Professor Siobhan B. Somerville argues that "the simultaneous efforts to shore up and bifurcate categories of race and sexuality in the late nineteenth century were deeply intertwined."[25] Lynching performances did not only regulate race relations, but also regulated gender relations.

As aforementioned, through Wells-Barnett's weekly newspaper, *Free Speech*, as well as in her pamphlets, *Southern Horrors: Lynch Law in All Its Phases* (1892), *A Red Record* (1895) and *Mob Rule in New Orleans* (1900) and other publications, Wells-Barnett became the first American, black or white, female or male, to expose lynching performances as white supremacist cultural production. Although her interdisciplinary examinations of lynching performances is often referred to as journalism, Wells-Barnett's weekly newspaper, pamphlets, speeches and books established a foundation for an interdisciplinary, critical cultural scholarship project, which can now be referred to as *critical lynching studies*. *Critical lynching studies* is herein identified as *an interdisciplinary critical cultural studies project examining lynching performance as extralegal, complex, cyclical and cross generational practices of white supremacist terrorism which ultimately functions to unjustly deny (primarily) African American victims their full wealth as United States citizens.* To identify Wells-Barnett's oeuvre as entre into *critical lynching studies* is to extend upon her black feminist legacy of producing cultural production functioning to clarify lynching as discursive and material whiteness performance. Wells-Barnett's activism did not only contest post-Reconstruction caricatures of black people as "bestial" used to justify the practice, but to "demand for justice to every citizen, and punishment by law for the lawless."[26] *Preaching the Blues: Black Feminist Performance in Lynching Plays* intends to function in the same way. *Preaching the Blues* facilitates further examinations of the structure and organization of lynching performances by supplementing its study with additional terms, cultural frameworks and analysis. Specifically, I intend to use anti-lynching drama, also known as lynching plays, as referential texts through which lynching performances can more easily be identified, thwarted, prosecuted and convicted, whenever, wherever and however they continue to be performed. In addition to their aesthetic function, lynching plays are also found to clarify lynching performances especially with regard to their structure as whiteness cultural performance in much the same way as Wells-Barnett's cultural production.

Wells-Barnett's journalistic examinations, especially *Southern Horrors*, provide a first cultural taxonomy making lynching more easily identifiable as acts of terrorism meant to keep blacks in their "place" as economically, politically and socially disadvantaged. By foregrounding lynching performance's intrinsic structure, Wells-Barnett shrewdly reframes lynching performances as whiteness cultural performance, counteracting a complex of intersecting whiteness narratives justifying its extralegal performance. *Southern Horrors* categorizes lynching performances' "phases" as follows: Chapter I: The Offense; Chapter II: The Black and White of It; Chapter III: The New Cry; Chapter IV: The Malicious and Untruthful White Press; Chapter V: The South's Position; and Chapter VI: Self Help.[27] In doing so, Wells-Barnett reframes lynching as whiteness cultural fiction (i.e. a prejudicial lie) which, in pursuit of American justice and lawfulness, should be challenged and prosecuted. She critiques the practice as "well known opposition growing out of slavery to the progress of the race," which when justified as "natural resentment of intelligence against a government of ignorance"[28] results in a slippery slope effect of a repeal of blacks' constitutional and civil rights as well as more lynching. In effect, Wells-Barnett concludes that there is no logical justification for lynching; any other explanation conceals a white, Southern ulterior motive, "this is a white man's country and the white man must rule."[29] Just as important, Wells-Barnett facilitates a paradigmatic shift of through which lynching performances can be read through an alternative (lens) thereby laying the groundwork for a "restaging" of the practice as anti-lynching playwrights would execute soon thereafter.

Due to an intricate nature of examining lynching as a whiteness cultural practice, it is necessary to frame the study of anti-lynching ideology as a critical endeavor. The term *critical lynching studies* is herein coined in order to help distinguish interdisciplinary, anti-lynching activism from the lynching performances themselves. It also forms a buffer around a term, "lynching," that is not only multivalent, but should not be used cavalierly without a trigger warning. Throughout *Preaching the Blues*, I use the term *lynching performances* as coined by performance studies scholar Kirk Fuoss[30] to refer to actual historical lynching resulting in torture and death, a point to which I will return. As aforementioned, I interchangeably use both terms *anti-lynching plays* and *lynching plays* to refer to the counter-hegemonic body of dramatic literature written to contest lynching performances.

Lynching dramas employ performance as a mode of language use, (as) a way of speaking. Lynching playwrights also use performance theory to engage theories of gender and place in dialogue with each other. In doing so, lynching plays must be fully considered for the ways they re-imagined lynching performance as a form of verbal art, "as a range of speech activity"[31] that could be inverted and re-purposed to both clarify truths about the whiteness performance practice while also purifying a black folklore tradition which was subject to contamination by minstrelsy and other performance-based misrepresentation and exploitation, including Jim Crow politics. Lynching plays function as repositories of black performance traditions, but more importantly, function epistemologically as a new and emerging ideology based upon black feminist performance. In these ways, lynching plays functioned as both archive of black folklore as well as a repertoire of black performance practices through which blacks could newly construct their social identities.[32] Since "the most challenging job that face the student of performance is establishing the continuity between the noticeable and public performance of cultural performances and the spontaneous, unscheduled optional performance contexts of everyday life"[33] I repeat and advance the work of previous scholars in clarifying how lynching plays function as a modern theatre form, seeking to both unmask white supremacist ideology in lynching performances as well as reform American theatre, especially with regard to representations of black people.

Finally, subsequent to a (relative) proliferation of critical/cultural examinations of anti-lynching campaigns that followed the publication and traveling exhibit of *Without Sanctuary: Lynching Photography in America* (2000), contemporary critical lynching studies scholars observe black women's representation as absent from (examinations of) material lynching culture, especially with regard to spectacle lynchings. In their review essay, "Looking at Lynching: Spectacle, Resistance and Contemporary Transformations," Cara Finnegan, A. Susan Owen and Peter Ehrenhaus note that a black woman subject is missing from interdisciplinary examinations of lynching culture despite the fact that it is she who was a likely subject of rape and/ or lynching. Finnegan, Owen and Ehrenhaus also claim that critical lynching studies scholars have been unsuccessful in returning black women to their examinations.[34] Unfortunately, *critical lynching studies* scholars have overlooked lynching dramas as repositories of black women's (feminist) performances, instead choosing to focus on literature,[35] photographs,[36] newspapers,[37] film[38] and even souvenirs.[39] In *Preaching the Blues*, black women are returned to material lynching culture through anti-lynching plays. Not only do anti-lynching plays facilitate black women's return to lynching culture, but her black feminist representation is found to perform using strategies *par excellence* disrupting, interrogating and sabotaging lynching performances as white supremacist cultural practice.

Preaching the Blues extends upon efforts to recover anti-lynching drama as a black feminist performance genre by foregrounding black feminist images and performance practices. Furthermore, *Preaching the Blues* uses black feminist performance theory to examine lynching plays based on their settings in black private settings versus white private settings thus remapping study of the genre away from an emphasis on the race and gender of the playwright to focus on the plays as interracial, cross generational performance. Examining lynching plays contingent upon race-based private settings are found to clarify respective black and white households' functionality as split subjects within an anti-lynching theatre tradition. Even further, such analysis of lynching plays makes possible a consideration of a complex of whiteness performance strategies otherwise unseen by those prohibited from entering whites only spaces. White women's performances in lynching plays are closely examined as active versus passive bearers of the lynching tradition. Finally, production of lynching plays on Historically Black College and University (HBCU) campuses is documented especially with regard to performing black feminisms. In *Preaching the Blues*, HBCUs are considered as a black performance saturated setting in which lynching drama can function affectively while at the same time functioning as a part of black feminist epistemology, pedagogy and praxis.

Preaching the Blues contrasts with critical lynching studies treatises seeking to return black women to lynching culture by literally increasing her visibility as a lynching victim. Whether as a photographic image or as a catalogue list of dead women's names, *Preaching the Blues* does not "presume benefits of political visibility" of public images of black women's victimization since "minorities and women can become victim to their own public representations, which contribute to rather than subvert dominant ideologies."[40] By foregrounding black women's performances in lynching plays, a (new) black women's subjectivity is positioned center stage, facilitating a discussion of "gender, color, nation and ethnicity" that bypasses essentialist categories to emphasize contingency rather than stability.[41]

As a difficult and emergent field of study, scholars of anti-lynching drama increasingly examine the dramatic genre as repositories of non-normative performance written by black women artists and intellectuals. However, there remains much to be done with regard to recovering the genre as an intercultural, cross generational performance-based contestation of white lynching performances. To limit the study of lynching plays to one of challenging representational images or as "a spectacle or 'a document' of black difference, instead of a cultural product requiring study in order to be grasped for its fullness"[42] limits study of the genre instead of expands it. To exclusively study images within a lynching play is to focus on theatre as an object as opposed to a process, as well as to deny how performance functions in cultural constructions of identity, gender, time and place. Therefore, *Preaching the Blues* advances the study of anti-lynching plays as (radical) black feminist modern performance theory.

It also must be noted that lynching plays prefigured or emerged as a contemporary of other avant-garde theatre movements, techniques and acting methods which were given sole credit for innovating many of the effects as also accomplished in lynching plays. As such, the genre's theoretical underpinnings as anti-lynching ideology should be foregrounded in order to make its mechanisms more legible. In addition to anticipating the field of performance studies which is traced to the 1960s, lynching plays are precursors and contemporaries of modern drama theories including Grotowski's poor theatre, Brecht's "alienation" effect (a-effect), Chamber Theatre technique as well as performance art. *Preaching the Blues* examines lynching plays written in "a variety of production styles,"[43] including black feminist Chamber Theatre method since the genre can be understood to exist with multiple existence and variation regarding to its form although it maintains an emerging continuity in content and function as cross generational, counterhegemonic performance.

Lynching drama remains an under-examined theatre genre; therefore, *Preaching the Blues* compares to a very small number of major titles including Kathy A. Perkins and Judith L. Stephens' *Strange Fruit: Plays on Lynching by American Women* (1999) as well as Koritha Mitchell's *Living with Lynching: African American Lynching Plays, Performance and Citizenship 1890–1930* (2012). In *Living with Lynching*, Mitchell foregrounds depictions of black households in lynching plays as environs in which black families practiced coping mechanisms used to deal with the effects of lynching. For Mitchell, lynching plays functioned as spaces where black women playwrights documented black families' experiences with lynching, affirming themselves and each other through the process of writing and sharing them. Mitchell's work extends to document lynching's absence from the archive[44] as well as to discuss the genre as a weapon in combatting black "shame" as institutionalized through the emergent forms practice, including America's prison industrial complex.[45]

In "Under Lynching's Shadow: Grimke's Call for Domestic Reconfiguration in *Rachel*," Anne Mai Yee Jansen, echo's Mitchell's examination of black households in lynching plays, comparing images in *Rachel* to those in American popular culture. Jansen reviews *Rachel* as a restructuring of the black household in response to lynching. In other words, Jansen examines *Rachel* as an expression of a non-normative family structure directly resulting from the ways lynching affects the Loving family. Jansen emphasizes Rachel's decision to forego marriage and children as her having chosen to "remain a child" instead of conforming to society's construction of womanhood. Jansen recognizes, however, how the image of Rachel challenges popular stereotypes of black women such as Mammy and Jezebel and in doing so, provides an alternative image of black women, families and black life.

Treva Lindsey's *Colored No More* (2017) considers lynching plays as part of an examination of non-traditional sources of black women's cultural production in Washington, D.C. According to Lindsey, lynching plays, stemmed, in part, from regular interaction between black Progressive era artists and intellectuals who met at the home of Georgia Douglas Johnson, also known as the S Street Salon, where they congregated as peers, friends and colleagues. Within the group, Lindsey focuses on prominent black women anti-lynching playwrights Georgia Douglass Johnson, Mary Burrill and May Miller as a collective who formed "a Negro woman's writing culture" by meeting each Saturday night. Lindsey astutely identifies the S Street Salon as "alternative political space in which women became central to lynching and anti-lynching narratives" as well as surveys the themes of the anti-lynching plays they wrote. By emphasizing black woman's return to material lynching culture as part of a black woman's art collective, Lindsey identifies lynching plays as "hitherto unnoticed space" within modern theatre's representational networks.[46]

Finally, in addition to reading lynching plays using performance methodologies, *Preaching the Blues* documents an ongoing production of lynching plays since 2012 as staged in black performance venues in the Deep South, U.S.A., specifically in and around Fort Valley State University in Georgia. As such, a real world experience and usefulness of lynching plays as performance episteme and praxis is foregrounded, especially as an artist response to the ongoing murder of young African Americans.

Chapter summaries

In Chapter 1, black feminist performance strategies are identified in lynching plays, especially with regard to intertextual readings with other black feminist cultural production. Using the lyrics to Bessie Smith's composition, "Preaching the Blues" (1927), as a performance-based framework, this chapter links the anti-lynching activism performance tradition to a blueswoman music tradition, specifically through use of a blues-spiritual aesthetic. Black feminist performance conventions such as non-normative performances of gender, sexuality, "motherhood" and a refusal of "the American dream" consistently recur whether examining literary genres written by highly literate black women teachers and artists or when analyzing blues music songs sung by imprisoned and/or blueswomen singers.[47] Chapter 1 also discusses the development of anti-lynching drama as early performance studies to conduct a close reading of Grimke's *Rachel*. Finally, Ida B. Wells-Barnett's anti-lynching activism is fore-grounded through an examination of the narrator-character in "Saving White Face,"[48] a black feminist Chamber Theatre adaptation of Bebe Moore Campbell's novel, *Your Blues Ain't Like Mine* (1992).

Chapter 2, subtitled "Examining Anti-Lynching Plays Set in White Households," focuses on black versus white private realms as split subjectivities in lynching plays. Several more anti-lynching plays are examined, more specifically, those that are set in white households, including Tracy Mygatt's *The Noose*, Corrie Crandall Howell's *The Forfeit* and May Miller's *Nails and Thorns*; there is also a comparative analysis of the black church version and the white church version of Georgia Douglas Johnson's *A Sunday Morning in the South*. Although subject based examinations of anti-lynching plays are now studied according to the race and gender of the author, this chapter proposes a re-mapping of the study of the plays based on setting. As such, anti-lynching plays are found to perform catharsis as clarification and purification in specific ways depending on the race of the household in which the play is set. Anti-lynching plays locate white households as principal sites in which the lynching cycle's preliminary, embedded and subsequent performances are performed. This chapter also uses a performance lens to consider the role of white women in lynching performances, especially with regard to their complicity in perpetuating white supremacist ideology.

Chapter 3 documents and analyzes performances of anti-lynching plays at Historically Black Colleges and Universities (HBCUs) especially with regard to Fort Valley State University's (GA) lynching play series as staged by the Joseph Adkins Players (JAP) student drama group between 2012 and 2019. Over the course of these several years, JAP recurrently staged "Saving White Face" (as aforementioned) as well as Georgia Douglas Johnson's *Safe* (c. 1929) in response to the murders of young black people including Trayvon Martin (2012), Reneisha McBride (2013), Michael Brown (2014), Tamir Rice (2014), John Crawford III (2014), Jordan Davis (2014) and others. This chapter conducts close readings of both Annie Nathan Meyer's *Black Souls* (1925), an anti-lynching play set on the campus of a black institution of higher learning, as well as Johnson's *Safe*. In this way, HBCUs are found to play an important part in preserving a black feminist, anti-lynching performance tradition through community and university theatre collaboration.

Notes

1 Patricia Schechter, *Ida B. Wells-Barnett and American Reform 1880–1930* (Chapel Hill, NC: University of North Carolina Press, 2001), 2.
2 Patricia Schechter, "Unsettled Business: Ida B. Wells Against Lynching or, How Antilynching Got Its Gender," in W. Fitzhugh Brundange (ed.), *Under Sentence of Death: Lynching in the South* (Chapel Hill, NC: University of North Carolina Press, 1997), 293–313.
3 Judith L. Stephens, "Lynching Dramas and Women: History and Critical Context," in Kathy A. Perkins and Judith L. Stephens (eds.), *Strange Fruit: Plays on Lynching by American Women* (Bloomington, IN: Indiana University Press, 1998), 3. Stephens' introduction also outlines the genre's distinction within American theatre, its significance as "womanist/feminist drama" and its principal conventions.
4 Marvin Carlson begins his overview of performance with this observation as made by Mary Strine, Beverly Long and Mary Hopkins in "Research, in Interpretation and Performance Studies: Trends, Issues, Priorities," in *Performance: A Critical Introduction* (London: Routledge, 1996), 1.
5 Stephens, "Lynching Dramas and Women," 11.
6 Marvin Carlson, *Performance: A Critical Introduction* (London: Routledge, 1996), 2.
7 Jane Blocker's analysis of Ana Mendieta's art using a performative lens in *Where Is Ana Mendieta? Identity, Performativity and Exile* (Durham, NC: Duke University Press, 1999), highly useful in articulating such a performance-based framework for the study of lynching drama.
8 Ibid, 14.
9 Stephens, "Lynching Dramas and Women," 5.
10 In *From Ritual to Theatre: The Human Seriousness of Play* (New York, NY: PAJ Publications, 1982), Victor Turner outlines a process through which a society's theatre emerged from its social drama proceeding through stages of breach, crisis, redress and either reintegration or recognition of schism.
11 Blocker, *Where Is Ana Mendieta*, 15.
12 See Treva Lindsey, *Colored No More* (Urbana, IL: University of Illinois Press, 2017).

13 Judith L. Stephens details Johnson's dramatic contributions in *The Plays of Georgia Douglas Johnson: From the New Negro Renaissance to the Civil Rights Movement* (Urbana, IL: University of Illinois, 2006).

14 In "Drama for Neglected People: Recovering Anna Julia Cooper's Dramatic Theory and Criticism from the Shadows of W.E.B. Du Bois and Alain Locke," *Journal of Dramatic Theory and Criticism* 27, no. 1 (Fall 2012), 25–50, Monica Ndounou discusses gender-based discrimination faced by Anna Julia Cooper with regard to access to black publications.

15 Stephens, *The Plays of Georgia Douglas Johnson*, 36–38.

16 Ibid, 37.

17 Ibid, 36.

18 Eileen Southern, *The Music of Black Americans: A History* (New York, NY: W.W. Norton and Company, 1983), 169–71.

19 Stephens, *The Plays of Georgia Douglas Johnson*, 186.

20 See "The Shout" in Southern's *The Music of Black Americans*, 169–71.

21 See "Signifying" by Claudia Mitchell-Kernan in Alan Dundes (ed.), *Mother Wit from the Laughing Barrel: Reading in the Interpretation of Afro-American Folklore* (Jackson, MS: University of Mississippi Press, 1990), 310–28.

22 Arthur F. Raper, *The Tragedy of Lynching* (Chapel Hill, NC: University of North Carolina Press, 1933), 481; Allen W. Trelease, *White Terror: The Ku Klux Klan Conspiracy and Southern Reconstruction* (New York, NY: Greenwood, 1972), quoted in James R. McGovern, *Anatomy of a Lynching* (Baton Rouge, LA: Louisiana State University Press, 1982), 2.

23 Dennis B. Downey and Raymond M. Hyser, *No Crooked Death* (Chicago, IL: University of Chicago Press, 1991), 3.

24 Lisa Duggan, "The Trials of Alice Mitchell: Sensationalism, Sexology and the Lesbian Subject in Turn-of the Century-America," in Kathleen Kennedy and Sharon Ullman (eds.), *Sexual Borderlands: Constructing an American Sexual Past* (Columbus, OH: Ohio State University Press, 2003), 165.

25 Siobhan B. Somerville, *Queering the Color Line: Race and the Invention of Homosexuality in American Culture* (Durham, NC: Duke University Press, 2000), 3.

26 Jacqueline Jones Royster (ed.), *Southern Horrors and Other Writings: The Anti-Lynching Campaign of Ida B. Wells, 1892–1900* (Boston, MA: Bedford Books, 1997), 50.

27 Ibid, 49–72.

28 Ibid, 60.

29 Ibid.

30 See Kirk Fuoss, "Lynching Performances, Theatres of Violence," *Text and Performance Quarterly* 19, no. 1 (January 1999), 1–37.

31 Richard Bauman, *Verbal Art as Performance* (Prospect Heights, IL: Waveland Press, 1977), 13.

32 Mitchell's reference to Diana Taylor's book *The Archive and the Repertoire* is from where this comes.

33 Bauman, *Verbal Art as Performance*, 28.

34 Cara A. Finnegan, A. Susan Owen, and Peter Ehrenhaus, "Review Essay: Looking at Lynching: Spectacle, Resistance and Contemporary Transformations," *Quarterly Journal of Speech* 97, no. 1 (February 2011), 100–13.

35 See Sandra Gunning's *Race, Rape and Lynching: The Red Record of American Literature 1890–1912* (New York, NY: Oxford University Press, 1996).

36 See Jonathan Markovitz's *Legacies of Lynching: Racial Violence and Memory* (Minneapolis, MN: University of Minnesota, 2004).

37 See James Allen, *Without Sanctuary* (Sante Fe: Twin Palms Publishers, 2000); Dora Apel and Shawn Michelle Smith, *Lynching Photographs* (Berkeley, CA: University of California Press, 2007); and Amy Louise Wood, *Lynching and Spectacle: Witnessing Racial Violence in America, 1890–1940* (Chapel Hill, NC: University of North Carolina, 2009).

38 See Susan Jean, "'Warranted' Lynchings: Narratives of Mob Violence in White Southern Newspapers, 1880–1940," *American Nineteenth Century History* 6, no. 3 (2005), 351-72.

39 See Harvey Young's essay, "The Black Body as Souvenir in American Lynching," *Theatre Journal* 57, no. 4 (2005), 639-57.

40 Blocker, *Where Is Ana Mendieta?* 25.

41 Ibid.

42 A. Yemisi Jimoh, "Mapping the Terrain of Black Writing During the Early New Negro Era," *College Literature: A Journal of Critical Literary Studies* 42, no. 3 (Summer 2015).

43 Perkins and Stephens, *Strange Fruit*, 4.

44 Koritha Mitchell, "Black Authored Lynching Drama's Challenge to Theater History," in *Black Performance Theory* (Durham, NC: Duke University Press, 2014), 87–98.

45 Koritha Mitchell, "No More Shame! Defeating the New Jim Crow With Anti-lynching Activism's Best Tools," *American Quarterly* 66, no. 1 (March 2014), 143–52.

46 Carlson, *Performance*, 2.

47 Here, I tie a blueswoman's music aesthetic to imprisoned black women as an out-growth of Sarah Haley's *No Mercy Here: Gender, Punishment and the Making of Jim Crow Modernity* (Chapel Hill, NC: University of North Carolina Press, 2016).

48 Since "Saving White Face" is unpublished, the play is framed by quotation marks instead of italics.

Bibliography

Blocker, Jane. 1999. *Where Is Ana Mendieta: Identity, Performance and Exile*. Durham, NC: Duke University Press.

Carlson, Marvin. 1996. *Performance: A Critical Introduction*. London: Routledge.

Cox, Delores. 2019. *www. workers. org*. January 7. www.workers.org/2019/01/07/after-more-than-100-years-congress-passes-an-anti-lynching-bill/.

Downey, Dennis B., and Raymond M. Hyser. 1991. *No Crooked Death*. Chicago, IL: University of Chicago Press.

Duggan, Lisa. 2003. "The Trials of Alice Mitchell: Sensationalism, Sexology and the Lesbian Subject in Turn-of-the-Century America." In *Sexual Borderlands: Constructing an American Sexual Past*, edited by Kathleen Kennedy and Sharon Ullman, 165–86. Columbus, OH: Ohio State University Press.

Fuoss, Kirk. 1999. "Lynching Performances, Theatres of Violence." *Text and Performance Quarterly*: 1–37.

Lindsey, Treva. 2017. *Colored No More: Reinventing Black Woman in Washington D.C.* Urbana-Champaign, IL: University of Illinois Press.

Markovitz, Jonathan. 2004. *Legacies of Lynching: Racial Violence and Memory*. Minneapolis, MN: University of Minnesota.

McGovern, James R. 1982. *Anatomy of a Lynching*. Baton Rouge, LA: University of Louisiana Press.

Mitchell, Koritha. 2014. "Black Authored Lynching Drama's Challenge to Theater History." In *Black Performance Theory*, edited by Thomas F. Defrantz and Anita Gonzalez, 87–98. Durham, NC: Duke University Press.

Mitchell-Kernan, Claudia. 1990. "Signifying." In *Mother Wit from the Laughing Barrel: Readings in the Interpretation of Afro-American Folklore*, edited by Alan Dundes, 310–28. Jackson, MS: University of Mississippi Press.

Ndounou, Monica. 2012. "Drama for Neglected People: Recovering Anna Julia Cooper's Dramatic Theory and Criticism from the Shadows of W.E.B. Du Bois and Alain Locke." *Journal of Dramatic Theory and Criticism*: 25–50.

Raper, Arthur F. 1933. *The Tragedy of Lynching*. Chapel Hill, NC: University of North Carolina Press.

Royster, Jacqueline Jones (ed.). 1997. *Southern Horrors and Other Writings: The Anti-Lynching Campaign of Ida B. Wells, 1892–1900*. Boston, MA: Bedford Books.

Schechter, Patricia. 1997. "Unsettled Business: Ida B. Wells Against Lynching or, How Antilynching Got Its Gender." In *Under Sentence of Death: Lynching in the South*, edited by W. Fitzhugh Brundage, 293–313. Chapel Hill, NC: University of North Carolina Press.

———. 2001. *Ida B. Wells-Barnett and American Reform 1880–1930*. Chapel Hill, NC: University of North Carolina Press.

Somerville, Siobhan B. 2000. *Queering the Color Line: Race and the Invention of Homosexuality in American Culture*. Durham, NC: Duke University Press.

Southern, Eileen. 1983. *The Music of Black Americans: A History*. New York, NY: W.W. Norton and Company.

Stephens, Judith L. 1998. *Lynching Dramas and Women: History and Critical Conxtext*. Bloomington, IN: Indiana University Press.

———. 2006. *The Plays of Georgia Douglas Johnson: From the Negro Renaissance to the Civil Rights Movement*. Urbana-Champaign, IL: University of Illinois Press.

Trelease, Allen W. 1972. *White Terror: The Ku Klux Klan Conspiracy and Southern Reconstruction*. New York, NY: Greenwood.

Turner, Victor. 1982. *From Ritual to Theatre: The Human Seriousness of Play*. New York, NY: PAJ Publications.

Chapter 1

A blueswoman matters

Black women's feminisms in anti-lynching plays

On February 21, 2019, Fort Valley State University's Joseph Adkins Players (JAP) student drama group performed Georgia Douglas Johnson's anti-lynching drama, *Safe* (c.1929), as part of the Douglass Theatre's inaugural Historically Black College and University (HBCU) art series.[1] Located in Macon, Georgia, some 30 miles away from Fort Valley State University's campus, the Douglass Theatre serves as a landmark performing arts venue for legendary Black music, theatre and film productions. "The Douglass," as it is locally known, was founded in 1911 by Charles A. Douglass, a black entrepreneur who channeled his knowledge of producing on the vaudeville circuit into the establishment as a thriving business. Charles Douglass served as a board member for the Theater Owners Booking Association (T.O.B.A.) circuit which was comprised of a chain of 40 black theatres through which black artists were booked as performers.[2] In addition to T.O.B.A. acts, many legendary performers played The Douglass including Ida Cox, Little Richard and Otis Redding. In 1925, Bessie Smith, one of the T.O.B.A.'s most successful acts, performed at The Douglass, soon followed by the "Mother of the Blues" Gertrude "Ma" Rainey who performed at the venue in 1927 and 1928.[3] In 2017, Douglass Theatre board members honored Ma Rainey, a native of Georgia, with its first plaque on the Douglass "walk of fame" in front of the theatre.

In addition to popular stage acts and productions, the Douglass once "hosted" another kind of cultural performance, as well. On August 1, 1922, John "Cockey" Glover's dead body was thrown into the lobby of the Douglass Theatre after a mob of an estimated 400 kidnapped Glover out of law enforcement's custody and killed him. Glover was subject to murder after shooting to death a white police officer and two others in a drunken brawl. Subsequent to his death,

Glover's nearly nude,[4] bullet riddled body was dumped in the lobby "to make a statement" directed at Charles Douglass, the successful black theatre owner.[5] Presumably, Glovers' lynched body served as a message to Mr. Douglass about what happens to blacks in Middle Georgia who didn't stay in their "place" with regard to economic and social success. Just like black bodies left hanging from bridges dividing segregated towns or in a heap on a county courthouse lawn, Glover's dead body performed as a display of "performance trace," a common "final act" of lynching performances which, according to performance studies scholar Kirk Fuoss, "functioned both to celebrate lynchings and to expand their potential for terrorizing large segments of the population."[6] In addition to corpses, other forms of "performance trace" included "placards and signs" as well as body parts which were also circulated as souvenirs.[7] Counteracting such whiteness remnants, a stone and bronze plaque now commemorates the acts of extralegal punishment taking Glover's life as well as the lives of 16 other local blacks and "those unknown." On October 22, 2016, the Episcopal Diocese of Atlanta commissioned the plaque and accompanying ceremony in order to foster "racial reconciliation."[8]

Like the plaque ceremony, the Joseph Adkins Players' 2019 production of *Safe* also performed as anti-lynching activism at the Douglass Theatre since it was the first anti-lynching play ever performed there. Although Johnson's play depicts events centered in and around the area, never before had *Safe* or any other anti-lynching drama been staged at the Douglass. JAP's onstage activism echoed that of the 2016 "pilgrims,"[9] taking place outside of the theatre, thereby reconciling a binary between onstage and offstage anti-lynching activist performances. Additionally, JAP's performance of *Safe* staged the effects of lynching performances on the local black community, especially the lynching of Sam Hose, a fellow Middle Georgian whose name does not appear on the commemoration plaque.[10] Finally, JAP's performance also facilitated catharsis in the Middle Georgia community by bringing together a diverse audience who could watch, think about and discuss the show. I will return to an examination of Georgia Douglas Johnson's *Safe* in Chapter 3, especially with regard to JAP's performance of the one-act play as part of its ongoing anti-lynching play series. Now, I tie JAP's performance to that of Bessie Smith whose song, "Preaching the Blues" provides a black feminist, performance-based framework for this book and chapter. Like Smith's song, JAP's staging of *Safe* performed within a black feminist, or non-normative, tradition. However, instead of "converting the souls" of vaudeville show attendees, JAP sought to "convert the souls" of audience members who would deny the effects of lynching on black households in Middle Georgia, those who minimize black feminist performance in the region or overlook the significance of HBCU art.

In her song "Preaching the Blues," Bessie Smith (1894–1937) writes and performs in a blueswoman tradition that Angela Davis identifies in *Blues Legacies and Black Feminisms* (1998) as "provocative," an "emergent feminist consciousness" among working class black communities representing a "politics of gender and sexuality . . . informed by and interwoven with their representations of race and class."[11] When Davis refers to Smith's song "Preaching the Blues" as an "atypical" blues song in which Smith "juxtaposes the spirit of religion and the spirit of the blues and contests the idea of an incontrovertible separateness of these two spheres," Davis highlights the song as a (liminal) performance in which Smith engages in black feminist play, combining sacred and secular realms in "an unprecedented combination of familiar elements."[12] In doing so, Davis echoes observations of esteemed music historian Eileen Southern who in *The Music of Black Americans* (1983) observes: "The dividing line between the blues and some kinds of spirituals cannot always be sharply drawn. Many spirituals convey to listeners the same feeling of rootlessness and misery as do the blues. . . . Some songs have such vague implications that they are classified as blues-spirituals."[13] The song "Preaching the Blues" explicitly performs as such a blues-spiritual composition, this time combining sacred performance traditions of a church preacher with a secular performance of women's intimate sex talk and a woman's seduction of a woman, "undermining the coherence of categories"[14] like the sacred and secular, constructing antagonistic relationships as noncontradictory oppositions,"[15] facilitating a reconsideration of both realms. As a blues-spiritual, Smith's performance challenges gender and sexuality norms. Like a preacher calling church worshippers to the altar, Smith calls the female listener, in the name of spiritual/sexual enlightenment, to convert from a position of ignorance about how to keep her man to a position of knowledge and understanding. In doing so, Smith sings each line like she is reading from a holy book of the blues, inviting her listeners to read with her and follow along. Finally, Smith switches perspective to that of an omniscient narrator who is watching the service as an outsider, embellishing the song with an image of Sister Green who "jumps up" to "do the shimmy," a provocative image that serves to further stimulate the listener/audience. By using performance tropes of the black church, Smith persuades/seduces her female audience to engage with her in order to gain a better understanding of the world. Smith uses the black spiritual performance tradition to perform a blues trope, the non-normative performance of sexuality among women. As such, in "Preaching the Blues," Smith creates a black feminist framework within which black women can overcome an ignorance (of how to keep a man) causing them to lose what they truly desire. Smith effectively reimagines the black church as a space in which black women can challenge gender performances to rehearse new ways of living, develop epistemologies of self-regard and express themselves more fully.

Like Bessie Smith's blueswoman performance, anti-lynching plays such as Georgia Douglas Johnson's *Safe* foregrounded black woman's subjectivity through a reconciliation of "epistemological, psychic and political binaries of Western metaphysics"[16] such as public versus private and art versus (political) activism. This chapter foregrounds representations of black women in lynching plays as well as identifying the performance strategies used by black women playwrights in anti-lynching plays to not only make black women visible within material lynching culture but through which a new black feminist subjectivity is created. Through this chapter's close examination of Angelina Weld Grimke's *Rachel* (1916) as well as "Saving White Face," a Chamber Theatre adaption of Bebe Moore Campbell's 1992 novel, *Your Blues Ain't Like Mine*, black women's images in anti-lynching plays are foregrounded as a model of a newly imagined American subjectivity. Among other black feminist strategies, anti-lynching dramatists are found to use: refusal (and sabotage), repetition, blueswoman aesthetics, occupant(y)ing, unmasking and interrogation of "the lynching story" to challenge white performance practices, especially those as established and reproduced through modern Jim Crow culture. Inasmuch as Jim Crow practices "made whiteness" through performances of segregation, consumerism, spectacle lynching, "domestic reconstruction" and other related "ritualistic enactment(s) of racial difference,"[17] anti-lynching plays are found to invert whiteness performance practices as representations of sites "of struggle against dominant racial and gender ideologies of nineteenth and early twentieth century America."[18] As performance or "representation without reproduction," black feminist ideology in lynching plays "can be seen as a model for another representational economy, one in which the reproduction of"[19] white supremacy is not guaranteed. Anti-lynching dramatists recombined discursive and

material elements of lynching performances to facilitate de-famil-
iarization (or alienation) of white supremacist norms from which
a novel, or new, modern dramatic genre emerged as well as a new
discursive subjectivity.

Finally, since the song "Preaching the Blues" is written about ten
years after Grimke's *Rachel,* and some 35 years after the publication
of both Ida B. Wells-Barnett's *Southern Horrors: Lynch Law in All
Its Phases* (1892) and Anna Julia Cooper's *A Voice From the South*
(1892), I reinforce a tie between a black feminist blueswoman tradition and the anti-lynching drama tradition using Julia Kristeva's
interpretation of Nietzche's "monumental time." Kristeva "valorizes
monumental time because it refigures time as a vast, all-encom-
passing undelineated field of temporality."[20] Therefore, in an anti-
lynching black feminist performance tradition "time is not linear
but circular, repetitive and cumulative."[21] Whether performed in
1926 by Bessie Smith at the Douglass Theater or in 2019 by Fort
Valley State University's Joseph Adkins Players in *Safe* or in the first
production of Grimke's *Rachel* in 1916, black feminist performance
traditions are found to repeat individually and collectively to contest emerging white supremacist performance practices, lynching and Jim Crow as violent systems "of gendered and racialized
economic exploitation and social control"[22] through which black
women are subject to oppression, exploitation, misrepresentation
and neglect.

The development of the anti-lynching
play genre

Anti-lynching plays by black women authors are one genre included
within a complex of interdisciplinary, black feminist discourse
beginning in the nineteenth century, including, as Lisa M. Anderson
chronicles in *Black Feminism in Contemporary Drama* (2008), "writings and speeches . . . of Anna Julia Cooper, Sojourner Truth, Maria
Stewart, Mary Church Terrell and Ida B. Wells-Barnett." Anderson
continues: "They understood the complex ways in which discrimination on the basis of race and sex affected their lives, and they worked
toward the dual goals of rights for women and blacks."[23] Black women
cultural producers responded to lynching performance as a material
and discursive practice of white supremacy through various modes of
communication including, but not limited to anti-lynching drama.
Theatre historian Perkins points out Grimke's early dramatic word

on lynching; however, black feminist artistic responses were multi-disciplinary and vast. According to Perkins,

> America heard of the horrors of lynching, not only from women playwrights in substantial numbers, but also from African American women in all areas of the arts. Visual artists, musicians, and choreographers such as Meta Vaux Warrick Fuller, Lois Malou Jones, Billie Holiday, Nina Simone, Katherine Dunham and Pearl Primus all contributed to exposing the brutality of lynching through their individual talents.[24]

Perkins' roll call identifies black feminist anti-lynching cultural production as a distinct art-activism tradition. Anti-lynching drama, therefore, constitutes a dramatic genre within a larger performance-based realm of interdisciplinary, anti-lynching activism. However, anti-lynching drama performs uniquely a black feminist approach to early modern drama. Anti-lynching dramatists experimented with both the technical realm of theatre involved in acting and staging techniques as well as ideological and political issues, especially with regard to visibility and representation. Through avant-garde theatre conventions, anti-lynching dramatists accomplished public challenges to white supremacist ideology without compromising their personal, physical safety.

Re-imagining theatre as a realm of public, black feminist intellectual thought

Mitchell traces black playwriting to blackface minstrelsy beginning in the 1850s[25] through a period of black popular theatre (1909–1932) to a (New Negro) era that called for black playwrights to produce black plays about black life. Mitchell notes that it was black performers, not black playwrights, who first established a successful black theatre as evidenced by its popularity among black audiences. Although these performers did not necessarily author the scripts that they acted out, they created a (theatre) space in which black writers could (re)imagine black performance, a necessary precursor to black playwriting. As M. Thompson observes, "Since 1900, the story of progress of the Black man in entertainment arts has been one of growing affirmation of manhood and full citizenship."[26] It should further be highlighted that a black woman, Anita Bush, established the first successful black theatre company, the Anita Bush Stock Company, later renamed the Lafayette Players, in which black theatre troupes employed black actors to produce (white authored) plays as seen on Broadway for black audiences. The success of the Lafayette Players as the immediate predecessor to the "New Negro" era effectively laid the groundwork for black theatre seeking to represent black people in a new way. Black theatre, therefore, is found to have been built upon the success of the minstrel and "popular" enterprises, as opposed to black-centered ideological foundations. Despite performances of racist caricatures of blacks as well as (re)producing the same white authored plays as those performed on Broadway, black theatre was not first defined by who wrote the play but by who was on stage and in the audience.

The development of dramatic literature by black authors emerged out of a vacuum among black artists and intellectuals who were not yet representing themselves through playwriting. Mitchell's historical analysis foregrounds a development of a black theatre based on both commercial theatre enterprises as well as dramatic criticism of high-profile cultural scholars (especially W.E.B. Du Bois and Alain Locke) who were in search of ways in which the black community could best represent their images on stage while also preserving their own folklore and cultural performances.[27] A focus on anti-lynching plays as a groundbreaking dramatic genre written by black women focuses on the plays' depiction of black households[28] as well as the collective environment into which they were birthed among black intellectuals and artists, especially in Washington, D.C.[29] When understood through a performance and performative paradigm, a major objective of *Preaching the Blues*, black households in anti-lynching plays are understood to foreground the black family's personal, affective ties while *at the same time* reinforcing the black household as a political realm in which readings of anti-lynching plays functioned as rehearsals of black feminist ideology counteracting lynching performances. Even further, since the home of Georgia Douglas Johnson (also known as the S Street Salon) served as a "literal and figurative home for black playwrights in the city"[30] collective acts of creating black dramatic art in black households are found to be "inseparable from complex discursive power relations"[31] in that they not only affirmed these households but, as indicated by Lindsey, also functioned as (informal) black institutions of higher order thinking.[32]

Black women's images in lynching plays also expressed new possibilities for black female subjectivity. As a distinct genre of American dramatic literature, anti-lynching plays directly countered "a complex" of narratives found in literature, on popular minstrel stages, in newspapers, in whiteness oral tradition and even through a newly emerging technology, film. Since Grimke's anti-lynching play directly responded to a lynching era which was (re)produced by D.W. Griffith's film, *Birth of a Nation* (1915), *Rachel* might be viewed as another movement of black feminist thought, with some Harlem Renaissance scholars marking the anti-lynching play as a starting point for the modern era.[33] Like the movements of black women's intellectual thought and cultural production directly preceding it, *Rachel* effectively reconstructed[34] a black woman's image in response to white supremacist discursive and material performance, specifically the lynching performance complex which included Jim Crow politics. In this instance, however, Grimke's black feminist performance-based response employed theatre as a direct response to lynching as whiteness cultural performance, not only as an appeal to audiences. In addition to representing black households as a space of reconciliation between the personal and political, Grimke effectively used theatre to negotiate Western metaphysics' private versus public binary spawning an anti-lynching drama movement soon joined by other emerging playwrights as well. Through her representation of a young black girl's private life and innermost thoughts, Grimke presents a radical black feminist ideology to the public without incurring a threat of lynching to which women who spoke out about the unjust practice were routinely subjected.[35]

Born in Boston, Massachusetts, as the only daughter of Archibald Grimke, a mixed-race man, and Sara Stanley, a white woman, Angelina Weld Grimke (1880–1958) came of age into relative privilege and prominence. Grimke's paternal grandmother, Nancy Weston, was a black woman slave who bore her master, Henry W. Grimke, three sons. Although he was born into slavery, Archibald Grimke's postsecondary education was eventually sponsored by his father's well-known sister, Angelina Grimke Weld (for whom he named his daughter), an abolitionist and feminist who with her sister Sarah were together known as the Grimke sisters. The second black man to graduate from Harvard Law School, Archibald Grimke raised his daughter Angelina alone after her mother committed suicide in 1898. As she expressed in her personal journals, the loss of her mother greatly affected Angelina Weld Grimke thereafter.[36]

After graduating from Boston Normal School of Gymnastics in 1902 and teaching physical education for five years, Grimke moved to Washington, D.C., to work as an English teacher at Armstrong Manual Training School. Grimke changed teaching positions to M Street High School (which later became known as Paul Laurence Dunbar High School) where Anna Julia Cooper was principal and Mary Burrill, another distinguished Harlem Renaissance era thinker and writer, also taught. Dunbar High, established in 1870, provided its black students with a high-quality education, graduating a veritable who's who of black American educators, artists, architects and leaders. May Miller, who went on to become a notable playwright herself, studied under Grimke while a student at Dunbar High. While a teacher at Dunbar, Grimke furthered her education by taking summer English courses at Harvard and writing poetry, fiction and literature reviews.

Anti-lynching drama's repetition

In *The Other Reconstruction: Where Violence and Womenhood Meet in the Writings of Ida B. Wells-Barnett, Angelina Weld Grimke, and Nella Larsen* (2000), Ericka M. Miller notes an array of subjects about which Grimke wrote poetry including "motherhood, despair, death, love between women, [and] love of fatherly figures." However, it is her writing about lynching that proves most compelling due to "their radical response to the dispossession of Black people as it manifested itself in the early decades of the twentieth century. For many of Grimke's works spoke of revolution."[37] In addition to poetry, Grimke penned short stories about lynching as well as her anti-lynching play, *Rachel*. Mitchell discusses revisions Grimke made to her play subsequent to its 1916 production, as well.[38] In fact, Grimke's repetitive use of lynching and motherhood as themes across her writing, no matter which genre, provokes multivalent comments from cultural scholars who refer to her writing as "fixated" or "obsessed." However, these observations are countered by Daylanne English's psychoanalytic reading in which she refers to Grimke's oeuvre, as well as the anti-lynching genre as a whole, as "allegories of domestic and political protest." English finds the "compulsion" in anti-lynching drama to be inherent to the genre as "a stark literary-formal and performative protest" comprised of "three most compelling – and interrelated – features" which are listed as:

> One, their psychoanalytic underpinnings; two, their function as specifically modern and literary forms of protest; and, three,

their linkage of lynching and black motherhood as symbolic and literal-that is psychosocial-structures . . . it is the sexuality and reproductive lives of modern black women that centrally concern Grimke and all of the other anti-lynching dramatists; neither their writings nor lynching itself can be understood apart from those concerns.[39]

Due to the "cross-generational trauma of lynching"[40] English concludes that black women authors of anti-lynching drama employed the plays as protest against the modernized racial and gender performances of oppression. According to English, repetition in *Rachel*, such as each scene taking place on the same day of the year, indicates the ongoing, cyclical nature of lynching-induced trauma inflicted upon black households. Unlike trauma in which the original injury is unknown to the victim, American blacks were, in fact, conscious of lynching as recurring events (albeit with multiple existence and variation) to which anti-lynching playwrights gestured by repeatedly writing anti-lynching plays. By using repetition across as well as within anti-lynching plays, New Negro women playwrights disrupted both masculinist constructions of a cultural subject as well as "white supremacist ideology . . . by a means of a combination of difference (a black female central subject) and sameness (repetition) . . . offering a sustained protest, with their repetitions serving to diagnose the nation rather than black women."[41] In doing so, black women anti-lynching playwrights did not only protest lynching performances by re-presenting a black (feminist) image, but these "early twentieth century African American writers had to reconstruct modernity itself."[42] Furthermore, a use of repetition in lynching plays is not only found to occur among these early black women playwrights but also in the anti-lynching play scholarship conducted by English, Stephens, Perkins, Mitchell, et al., as well as in my own staging of the plays which is a point to which I return.

Black feminist dramatic theory and anti-lynching drama

When W.E.B. Du Bois established an NAACP drama committee in 1916, he took the anti-lynching activism as published in *The Crisis* a step further. In *Art in Crisis: W.E.B. Du Bois and the Struggle for African American Identity and Memory*, Amy Helene Kirschke describes how Du Bois used "the magazine to document the violence in graphic detail. . . . He published accounts of lynchings, eyewitness descriptions and photographs of lynching victims. Political cartoons in the magazine depicted the horrors of lynching."[43] Additionally, Du Bois published anti-lynching plays. Even more significantly, the NAACP drama committee selected Grimke's *Rachel* as its premier production, "the first black-authored, nonmusical drama to be executed by black actors for a broad audience."[44] However, Du Bois' instrumentality in getting *Rachel* produced does not belie the fact that *Rachel*'s aesthetic and ideological sensibilities are more closely tied to those of Anna Julia Cooper (1858–1964) who was a principal at Paul Laurence Dunbar High School when Grimke began teaching there. According to theatre and film scholar Monica Ndounou, Angelina Weld Grimke's anti-lynching play, *Rachel*, is more easily traced to Anna Julia Cooper's earlier dramatic theories, as opposed to those of Du Bois or Locke. In "Drama for Neglected People: Recovering Anna Julia Cooper's Dramatic Theory and Criticism from the Shadows of W.E.B. Du Bois and Alain Locke," Ndounou refers to Cooper's dramatic theory as "dramaturgical meritocracy," which encompasses "the practice and process of emphasizing the intrinsic value of 'neglected people' and advocating human rights, social justice and full rights of American citizenship,"[45] directly linking Cooper's dramatic theory to Grimke's lynching play. According to Ndounou, Cooper[46] found to be the first scholar to outline a theory of black drama through which an audience's higher order thinking skills could be engaged and to which *Rachel* is more closely tied, especially through its performative aesthetics.

As evidence for her argument, Ndounou analyzes Cooper's oeuvre including her creative work as well as her dramatic criticism including "observations of popular audience expectations and recurring role types and performances"[47] to unearth how "Cooper uses drama and related means to advocate for human rights, social justice and full rights of American citizenship."[48] According to Ndounou, Cooper's premise of "dramaturgical meriotocracy" proceeds from the following three components:

1) The merging of art for art's sake as well as the use of art as propaganda, 2) a form of "self-consciousness" in terms of self-perception in conflict with externally imposed identity, 3) the pedagogical function of drama to serve as a process of Americanization,

setting the tone for Grimke's *Rachel*. Ndounou further explains how Cooper's close reading of popular representational images of black people, especially Uncle Tom's Cabin, "alludes to the links between representation and its political stakes in her work." Although a discussion of black women's images at first seems to be absent as "an oversight of the early Black feminist,"[49] Ndounou highlights Cooper's use of "the terminology of stage directions to indirectly call for the Black woman" to self-produce her own image as strong evidence for a black feminist dramaturgical theory, especially through her assertion: only the black woman can say "when and where I enter, in the quiet, undisputed dignity of my womanhood without violence and without suing or special patronage, then and there the whole Negro race enter with me."[50] Ndounou's emphasis on Cooper's "dramaturgical meritocracy" as black feminist performance theory upon which anti-lynching plays are based does the all-important work of emphasizing black feminist theory as fully formed ideology through which to contest white supremacy. Even further, Ndounou finds Cooper's black feminist performance theory to function as pedagogy in the practice of American radical democracy and citizenship. Although often overlooked due to the non-traditional ways in which it was documented, Cooper's dramatic theory and criticism suggested a performance-based strategy for effectively creating and projecting an image of merit (as opposed to respectability) in a society seemingly hell bent on discrediting black people.

Black feminist performance theory in anti-lynching plays

Inasmuch as Angelina Weld Grimke's *Rachel* challenges dominant ideologies of race and gender through an anti-lynching play, Cooper's theory of "dramaturgical meritocracy" should be enlarged to encompass other anti-lynching dramatists, such as Georgia Douglas Johnson, Tracy Mygatt, May Miller and others, since the dramatic genre generally performs according to Cooper's framework. Individually and collectively, black women dramatists especially used anti-lynching plays to contest discursive and material performances making up lynching's "performance complex" or "the entire web of performance woven in and around lynchings."[51] *Rachel* constitutes the earliest effort of a black woman using drama "as a weapon of social change"[52] in a fight against emerging white supremacist ideology as reproduced through intersecting narrative realms. In the same way black feminist fiction writers such as Pauline Hopkins and Frances

Harper deployed novels some 20 years prior, Grimke used drama to "reconstruct" black women's image. This time, however, Grimke crafts a non-normative image of black women through which a complex, performance-based theory of race and gender ideology could be enacted, albeit controversial. Due to grotesque portrayals of black women's images rendering her subjectivity as "invert(ed): perverse, primitive, and pathological and therefore unentitled to protection or freedom,"[53] Grimke's *Rachel* uses anti-lynching drama as a challenge to intersecting race- and gender-based constructions in a way that disrupts white cultural production. Not only is Grimke faced with racial constructions of black people as "grinning darkies" per the popularity of blackface minstrelsy and spectacle culture, but she must also contend with gender constructions of women excluding her, which is compounded by a lack of solidarity from white women who contradict themselves when advocating for women's rights such reproductive rights and anti-rape activism.[54] Besieged by such heavy burdens, Grimke is subject to criticism for directing her dramatic message to a white audience as evidenced by her Victorian cultural references, melodramatic writing style as well as Rachel's non-normative image as an unmarried "mother of unborn children" and a black woman intellectual. Grimke's Rachel accomplishes her new subjectivity by refusing the American dream of marriage and childbirth, a black feminist response to white supremacist performance of lynching not found to be in keeping with performances of highly trained, well-educated women of mixed race heritage who, in the spirit of a "cult of true womanhood," supposedly endeavored to exemplify "domesticity, submissiveness, purity and piety"[55] On the contrary, Grimke's *Rachel* shuns such "true womanhood" ideals, instead performing a "refusal" of white supremacist ideology, a radical black feminist act more likely to be practiced by imprisoned black women who "challenged the politics of respectability," seeking to disrupt race and gender-based systems of oppression.[56] Neither does Grimke represent black women's folklore nor traditional performance practices using dialect or humor. Instead, *Rachel's* black feminist performance is centered upon her sober and serious[57] demeanor. Offstage, black women were routinely imprisoned or lynched for such open displays of resistance of white supremacy. Onstage, *Rachel* represents a young black woman's individual performance of black feminist resistance practices. Although her activism is not public spectacle, her private performance might even be more effective since she disrupts a (lynching) cycle of black oppression on her own terms, as opposed to terms provoked by the dominant society for which she, as a black woman in the Jim Crow era,[58] would undoubtedly suffer unspeakable reproach.

Re-imagining black women's subjectivity

Angelina Weld Grimke's *Rachel* depicts the effects of lynching on a black household, specifically with regard to its effects on its black woman dramatis personae. *Rachel* also depicts the logic used in reconstructing the black household as a black private domain through which black feminist cultural production is performed. The three-act play, which is noted to be akin to the structure of Ibsen's "A Doll's House,"[59] is centered upon the coming of age of Rachel Loving who matures from a high school aged teenager to a young woman of marriage and childbearing age while actively rejecting a white supremacist society's family construct. The lessons upon which Rachel's intellectual, social and physical maturation occur are based on racist experiences she herself deals with as well as those she watches her family, friends and acquaintances endure. Rachel performs a process of critical thinking that yields an emotional transformation from which she emerges as a non-normative subject who is unwilling to replicate a white supremacist societal/family construct. Consequently, Rachel refuses to reproduce white supremacy in both physical and ideological senses; instead choosing to create her own black feminist ideology in which she performs as non-normative mother.

Rachel Loving is introduced in Act One as the bright, young, energetic daughter of a hardworking seamstress, Mrs. Loving, who is the sole provider for her and her older brother, Tom. Mrs. Loving's age and physical labor cause ailments and exhaustion, perhaps indicating Mrs. Loving's status as an "overworked and underpaid" head of household due to her husband's absence.[60] The flat in which the Loving family resides reflects their humble yet stable class position as educated, working poor African Americans. Although their furnishings are "plain," the décor is well kept and coordinated with the colors green and white, "a bookcase full of books," as well as classic and modern paintings. As noted by Judith Stephens, most black women authored plays take place in black homes which reflects a "high value black women have always placed on home maintenance and family life" as well as,

> juxtapos(es) . . . the brutal public act of lynching with the private, intimate atmosphere of the home creat(ing) a theatre of jarring

contrasts and incongruity for those who idealize the "American home" by equating it with an atmosphere of safety and peace.[61]

At first, neither Rachel nor Tom seem to be too adversely affected by the economic status of the household since they both display gregarious natures as young people looking forward to promising futures. In fact, Rachel radiates an expansive if not boundless energy and creativity for life and motherhood, expressions that are established by her returning home late after stopping to play with a very young boy who has just moved into the apartment building. Even further, while practicing the piano as part of music lessons, Rachel chooses to play a standard lullaby, further indicating her love of art and education geared toward the well-being of children. She stops her lesson to emphasize to her mother a "lovely" lyric which admonishes its baby subject, "Only don't forget to sail, Back again to me. (pauses in hushed tones) Ma dear, it's so beautiful-it-it hurts." Rachel strongly establishes her inclination to protect, educate and create on behalf of children, especially the "brown and black babies" she prays to God to conceive every night.

Rachel's attempts to enchant and engage her mother are unsuccessful however when Rachel repeatedly asks about her mother's seemingly sad demeanor. Mrs. Loving avoids Rachel's inquiries, finally distracting her daughter with a request to run an errand to pick up dinner. We are not made aware of the actual cause of Mrs. Loving's distress until Rachel returns with a surprise guest. Rachel returns to the apartment with Jimmy, the little boy from downstairs who was the source of her distraction the first time she returned home late. Instead of greeting the child warmly, Mrs. Loving reacts to him as if she's seen a ghost, prompting Mrs. Loving to finally disclose what's been bothering her. Upon Mrs. Loving's revelation to Rachel and Tom about the circumstances surrounding her widowhood, their fatherlessness and the family's subsequent move North, Act One ends. Rachel and Tom find out that their family's migration resulted from the lynching of their father and half-brother. Mrs. Loving retells the story of their father and half-brother's murder through which the adolescents learn that their father was lynched for publishing in his well-respected newspaper a "most terrific denunciation" of a mob that knowingly lynched an innocent black man for a crime committed by a white man. Mrs. Loving's narration thereby fulfills Stephens' third criteria of a woman's retelling of events.[62] Upon hearing "the lynching story" of her own father's death, Rachel begins to think logically about the position of black mothers throughout the South as well as the fate of black children who, like her half-brother, would be subject to lynching upon maturation. Upon Rachel's critical examination of lynching's discursive and material practices, she applies her analysis to her own performance as a member of American society, especially regarding the way she serves the children around her. Rachel "thinks out loud" when she shares her thought process with her mother:

Rachel:	I understand, Ma dear. (a silence. Suddenly) Ma, dear, I am beginning to see – to understand – so much. (slowly and thoughtfully) Ten years ago, all things being equal, Jimmy might have been George? Isn't that so?
Mrs. Loving:	Why, yes, if I understand you.
Rachel:	I guess that doesn't sound very clear. It's only getting clear to me, little by little. Do you mind my thinking out loud to you?

Rachel logically reasons that black mothers throughout the South live in anguish and sleeplessness over the fate of their children. In a monologue that lies at the heart of Rachel's appeal to white mothers,[63] Rachel concludes, "It would be more merciful – to strangle the little things at birth. And so this nation – this white Christian nation – has deliberately set its curse upon the most beautiful – the most holy thing in life – motherhood! Why-it-makes-you-doubt-God!" Rachel thereby denounces lynching performance as America's principal narrative on the basis that it curses motherhood, making her question not only Christianity but the idea that God exists. Rachel's reference to infanticide as a remedy to lynching's curse on motherhood, (indirectly) repeats a trope embodied by Margaret Garner's story in which she kills her child rather than allow her to live as a slave.[64] Grimke also later repeats the theme of black motherhood as a curse in her 1919 short story, "The Closing Door," in which Grimke also theorizes "colored mothers [as] . . . unlike white mothers, [since they] must live with the fear that their children are vulnerable to mob violence which continues to thrive with the support of white women."[65] Having reached such an anti-Romantic conclusion about black motherhood, Rachel experiences a nervous collapse; she faints into her mother's arms never to be the same carefree girl again.

In Act Two it is four years later to the date and Rachel has adopted Jimmy after his parents succumb to illness. Although they've successfully completed post-secondary education programs as leaders of their classes, both Tom and Rachel are unemployed, indicating a racist suppression of their economic opportunities as a by-product of lynching. Unlike her disposition as a young teenager, Rachel's manner is now sober, lacking naiveté. She insists that she "sees things the way they are"[66] versus the "pessimism" or "morbidity" of which John Strong, Tom's associate and her potential suitor, accuses her. Strong asserts that he will take her out to the theatre in order to take her mind off things, a gesture Rachel rebuffs through her observation that he talks to her "as though she were a jellyfish," layering in a critique of Jim Crow segregation of theatre audience: "Some of these theatres put you off by yourself as though you had leprosy. I'm not going."[67] Here, again we see Rachel's criticism of society's "everyday" racist practices that pervade all its realms as well as her display of an unwillingness to stay in her "place" as a thinking black woman.[68] Although she explicitly resists his charms, Strong's goodbye kiss into her open palm incites a Romantic daydream in Rachel which only is interrupted by Mrs. Lane and Ethel, a woman and her child who are seeking to rent a vacant apartment. Mrs. Lane needs to move Ethel to a new school due to cruel treatment from a teacher and students at her former school which has caused Ethel serious emotional distress. Rachel can't help but notice the child's complete withdrawal when Ethel refuses to engage with her as an innocent child would. Even worse, Jimmy returns home from school with his own tale of having been terrorized by a group of young white boys who call him a "nigger" while throwing rocks. Consequently, Rachel falls deeper into despair about the lifelong racist "torture" faced by black people, an ordeal that does not even spare small children. Rachel lashes out against God, declaring her creative power more merciful than his due to the prolonged way he administers death. Rachel experiences a complex "crisis of freedom and disruption of continuity"[69] as typically performed by modern subjects who express "doubt and skepticism – of religion, society, politics, ethics and art itself . . . leaving modern dramatic characters existentially bereft and unhinged."[70]

Rachel's existential crises reaches an all-time high in Act Three in which we find her totally immersed in creating a world for the children in her life even while she physically and emotionally seems ill. Rachel is dedicated to elaborate storytelling and extended childcare in spite of the fact that her mother recently found her unconscious, leaving her bedridden for several days. John Strong returns to visit her, this time confronting her about her "strange" behavior. When Rachel discloses to him her recent thoughts, especially how her unborn children have come to her in her dreams begging not to be born, he accuses her of having lost her "self-control" and attempts to convince her to marry him. Strong performs an extended monologue in which he describes a home he has bought and meticulously furnished with her in mind. In this way, Strong attempts to seduce Rachel with a material life with which he thinks she can preoccupy herself and presumably live "happily ever after." John's overtures almost work until the couple is interrupted by the sound of Jimmy crying due to recurring nightmare's he's endured since encountering the older white boys. Jimmy's cries return Rachel to her nervous state in which she refuses John's proposal. Rachel sends John away after she remembers that the life John promises only offers more heartache and torture which she is determined not to experience. Rachel, who has come to value "inner self possession and fulfillment, rather than outward appreciations and possession,"[71] which she defines as soothing the physical and psychic wounds of her little Jimmy and other children who are always already subject to society's racist torture. Mothering children already born is what Rachel determines to be "right" even in the midst of so many whiteness immoralities. Rachel sacrifices the American dream of marriage and motherhood as meaningless in order to attend to Jimmy's nightmares, consciously avoiding a Romantic narrative tied to a ritual torture of black bodies. In doing so Rachel creates her own world, "epitomizing individualistic self-expression,"[72] which is driven by her own (black feminist) ethics and morals.

As modern theatre, Grimke's *Rachel* effectively purifies the black household, transfiguring it from a realm of white ritual defilement into an intellectual domain in which black feminists engage in critical thought in order to resist and/or subvert lynching culture. *Rachel* (and lynching plays set in black households following it) provides redress for Mary Church Terrell's 1904 observation: "The Negro's home is not considered sacred by the superior race. White men are neither punished for invading it nor lynched for violating colored women and girls."[73] Through her refusal to marry and bear children, Rachel purges her household of the means to reproduce white supremacist ideology. Grimke uses theatre as a public expression of black feminist thought which is cultivated within in a private setting, a black household. The black household is the setting in which black feminist ideology is not only theorized but practiced/performed.

Rachel also reimagines black households as a liminal space where black children can safely play to find comfort and refuge from the racist society into which they were born and then psychologically and physically tortured on public streets and in public institutions. As such, Rachel performs as a black feminist ideological and cultural producer, a process to which the audience is privileged. In this way, Grimke's play reconciles a false binary of public and private, an assumption upon which white supremacy, as a Western ideology, is based. Although Rachel engages in intellectual activity in the privacy of the Loving household, she enacts her black feminist ideology through her refusal to marry and bear her own children, her nontraditional mothering "of the unborn,"[74] as well as her formal and informal adoption of black children who live nearby. Consequently, Rachel's image as non-normative mother challenges the Mammy figures, who according to Grace Elizabeth Hale were

> in an important sense white fictions of black womanhood. As markers of both class status and as the conduits through which these identities were reproduced within white children, mammies reinforced the fiction of continuity that legitimated the new southern white middle class.[75]

The Mammy narrative is found to function as an intersectional cultural fiction that helped to effectively "solidify white women's particular gender formation"[76] as "southern lady" since she was "key to the paradox of white women empowered by an image of weakness."[77] In counteracting the Mammy image, *Rachel* contests white supremacist ideology as principally reproduced by white women in novels.

Counteracting the Mammy image sets up lynching plays to create a new image of a black mother subject. Lynching plays such as *Rachel* can be classified as abusurdist since they are "marked from its beginning with a preoccupation with birth and reproduction."[78] Lynching plays in black households deal with first-hand effects of lynching on black families, especially black mothers. However, depictions of black mothers in lynching plays are found to perform non-normatively. Black mothers in anti-lynching plays are not strictly defined by cultural norms such as physically giving birth or possessing "a mother's instinct." As a black feminist subject, Rachel breaks race and gender identity categories, especially that of biological "mother." Rachel's obsession with providing black children with pleasant thoughts and dreams counteracts the real nightmares by which black children are terrorized within the social and political realms of white supremacist culture. Even further, Rachel's obsession marks her performance of motherhood as based on lynching's inversion of morality as, "outside or at least on the tenuous edge of legibility." Even though Rachel's *avant-garde* identity as modern mother is not "false," it "challenges the coherence of that presumed real."[79] Like Grimke's aforementioned obsession with lynching as a literary theme, Rachel's obsession with facilitating "sweet dreams" for the children with whom she interacts represents a cross generational trauma black children have endured since slavery. Through Rachel, Grimke indicates performance as "representation without reproduction;"[80] in this case, Rachel's identity of mother is performative as opposed to biological/cultural. As such, *Rachel* "configures" Grimke's work "as something more than a theatrical performance, it helps reinforce the claim that the work actually makes something happen."[81] Although *Rachel* may not have persuaded lynchers to cease and desist with performing the whiteness cultural practice, Grimke's play did succeed in inspiring other aspiring writers to compose dramatic literature both within and outside of the anti-lynching play tradition.[82]

Rachel's non-normative depictions of a black woman and motherhood did not relieve Grimke of the same accusations of "sentimentalism," or characterization as avoiding "the uglier details of life, illustrating the 'mutual tenderness, affection and solicitude' to be found in domesticity and advocate submission to authority as a means of achieving Christian salvation" as had been levied against earlier black women fiction writers who were also thought to have been imitating a sentimental style made popular by white women writers of the late eighteenth and nineteenth century.[83] Scholars reviewing Grimke's work overlook *Rachel* as a reconciliation of European and black American aesthetics as well as sacred and secular traditions in which black feminist performance practices are juxtaposed with white ideological constructs in order to create a new black feminist social subject.

Not only does *Rachel* function epistemologically, but by depicting a black woman engaged in creating a non-normative performance, the play also functions pedagogically by teaching its audience how to creatively respond to lynching. In the same way that Anna Julia Cooper conceptualized and used dramaturgical meritocracy as a pedagogical tool in fostering "citizenship, democracy and Christian ideals" among blacks, Grimke instructs her audience on a process of resisting white supremacy. Rachel effectively models a refusal of marriage and motherhood as a principle strategy of anti-lynching performance.

In conclusion, black women's return to lynching culture fits into no pre-existing narrative mold, even so-called natural ones, such as "mother," challenging gender performance norms. In fact, black women's return to "the lynching story" is so novel that critical lynching studies scholars ignore or misread her, even when they encounter her. Lynching plays, on the contrary, feature entirely new images of black women such as *Rachel's* "childless mother." As an image of black women, *Rachel* effectively reconstructs images of black women as well as that of the black domestic sphere, in general. Not only does *Rachel* challenge race and gender norms, but also class norms tied to a "politics of respectability" as espoused by early twentieth-century black clubwomen's movements. On the contrary, *Rachel's* refusal of the American dream is more closely tied to imprisoned women and blueswomen singers, like Bessie Smith, who unapologetically "preached the blues" about lynching and the repressive conditions of Jim Crow modernity, thereby reconciling any social or economic class distinction between performance strategies practiced by black feminists.

"Saving White Face" – black feminist Chamber Theatre adaptation as anti-lynching drama

In this section, I examine the performance-based strategies used in "Saving White Face," an anti-lynching play using Chamber Theatre technique to adapt Bebe Moore Campbell's novel *Your Blues Ain't Like Mine* (1992) and Gwendolyn Brooks' poem, "A Bronzeville Mother Loiters in Mississippi. Meanwhile, a Mississippi Mother Burns Bacon" (1960). In "Saving White Face," Chamber Theatre technique, a method of adapting literary texts to stage developed by Robert Breen (1909–1991), is used as a performance methodology, thereby returning the black woman subject to discursive and material lynching culture. "Saving White Face" performs in "a 21st century black feminist dramatic aesthetic. . . (to) construct and reconstruct history and identity . . . revealing an otherwise hidden history, a black feminist history that centers women's lives and experiences."[84] "Saving White Face" also recovers anti-lynching dramatists as American theatre practitioners "in contrast to the traditional erasure and denigration of (black) women as speakers, performers and teachers"[85] as well as public intellectuals, dramatists and cultural theorists.

"Saving White Face's" black woman narrator-character, "Ida," is rendered legible to all who overlook, ignore and misread her black feminist contributions. In keeping with other counter-hegemonic strategies performed in anti-lynching dramas, such as reframing lynching photographs and (re)interrogating and unmasking "the (archetypal) lynching story," "Saving White Face" uses Chamber Theatre's narrator-character convention, a blues aesthetic and "mirroring" between split black and white woman subjects to (re)present a black woman subject, "Ida," within lynching culture from which she is exiled. Also, as a critical intervention of Chamber Theatre method, this section analyzes "Saving White Face" as black feminist revision of Chamber Theatre method.

Re-interrogating "the lynching story"

"Saving White Face's" plot depicts a version of an "archetypal lynching story" as Patricia Schechter references the whiteness narrative in "Unsettled Business: Ida B. Wells Against Lynching, or How Antilynching Got Its Gender."[86] In "the lynching story," a "fragile, innocent" white female victim needs to be protected/rescued by a gallant white male hero from rape by a villainous black man. Black women are absent from "the lynching story." As an everyday whiteness discursive performance, "the lynching story" institutionalizes a "system of economic exploitation and social control" based in gender and race ideology,[87] a point to which I will return. Although Campbell's epic novel fictionalizes Emmett Till's 1955 murder, including the lives of both the African American and white families who were directly affected by it for 30 years afterward, "Saving White Face" focuses only on the white household of the lynchers, the Cox family, effectively marking it, through domestic violence, as a "preliminary lynching performance site."[88]

In "Saving White Face" the drama unfolds around Lily Cox, a white female high school dropout, who, while "innocently" satisfying a "curiosity," sneaks into a pool hall that her husband, Floyd, owns. While snooping around among the black male laborers who patronize the establishment, she overhears a young black boy speaking French although he doesn't seem to be speaking directly to her. Her husband, Floyd, finds out about the encounter, violently smacking her, admonishing her to neither go into the juke joint again, nor to let their family find out about it. He reminds her: "You know how Daddy and them are." Despite Floyd's warning, Floyd's father does find out about the incident and pressures Floyd to handle it, "like you was one of us." Floyd, his father and brother, who constitute a mob, lynch the boy. The murder receives national attention when Clayton Pinochet, a liberal minded son of the town's wealthiest family, secretly calls a friend and fellow journalist to cover the story for a New York newspaper. This depiction of the events leading up to and immediately follow the murder reflect Kirk Fuoss' "preliminary, embedded and subsequent," classes of the lynching performance cycle.[89] "Ida," a black woman who is a composite character from the novel, narrates the staged drama and also "doubles" as two white male patriarchs.

A traditional, American (hegemonic) narrative device, "the lynching story" is used to justify the disproportionate lynching of African Americans, especially during "the lynching era," or the period between 1865 and 1930.[90] "The lynching story" functions as a master narrative of white supremacy constructing race and gender in specific ways. Although it constitutes a cultural fiction, "the lynching story" stands as a primary reference informing American social, political and economic relations. "The lynching story" transmits orally, through newspapers, ballads, photographs, on theatre stages as well as through Hollywood film, like *Birth of a Nation*.[91] Even further, the discursive and material practice stands at the center of American literature analyzed by Trudier Harris in *Exorcising Blackness: Historical and Literary Lynching and Burning Rituals* (1984) as well as Hazel Carby's *Reconstructing Womanhood: The Emergence of the Afro-American Woman Novelist* (1987). According to Sandra Gunning, "the lynching story" emerged after Reconstruction,

> (when) the idea of the black rapist proved particularly useful for white Americans seeking to come to terms with post-Civil War anxieties over national unity, black emancipation, altered gender roles, growing labor unrest, European immigration, and the continued evolution of the United States into an increasingly multiethnic nation.[92]

In *Race, Rape and Lynching: The Red Record of American Lynching* (1996), Gunning recounts this development of "the lynching story," including its "deployment as a metaphor in the construction of racial identities in literature in the late nineteenth and early twentieth centuries."[93] The "black brute," as referred to by Gunning, is perhaps the most popular subject to emerge from this fiction and is still used to justify the disproportionate incarceration and murder of black males until today.[94]

Gwendolyn Brooks directly references the "black brute" image in her poem, "A Bronzeville Mother." "Saving White Face" incorporates the reference when Ida and Lily simultaneously perform the text in the following (excerpted) way:

Ida and Lily:	But there was a something about the matter of the Dark Villain.
Lily:	He should have been older perhaps.
Ida:	The fun was disturbed, them all but nullified When the Dark Villain was a blackish child of fourteen, with eyes too young to be dirty, And a mouth too young to have lost every reminder of its infant softness.

Through Brooks' poem, Lily critically examines the image of the black brute in "the lynching story," contrasting the narrative with her real life encounter with a not so dark skinned adolescent who is too young to possess the beast-like qualities ascribed to the Dark Villain. Lily's performance in "Saving White Face" contrasts the image of her as incapable of critical thought as "the lynching story" infers. On the contrary, "Saving White Face" depicts Lily as a "knower,"[95] a subject fully capable of higher order thinking about her positionality as well as that of (O)thers.

In contrast to black men's hyper violent images, black women are wholly absent from "the lynching story." Black women's absence from the "the lynching story" constitutes an "exile" invoking "disappearance, movement and interdeterminancy,"[96] launching her into a non-normative, or queer, subjectivity. As an exile, black women are therefore rendered invisible, unstable and incomprehensible. "Saving White Face's" narrator-character, "Ida," therefore represents a black woman's "multi-spatial and multi-temporal"[97] return to "the lynching story." This maneuver reverses institutionalized racism and sexism exiling her, thereby denying her contributions. Now, "Saving White Face's" "Ida" renders black women not only visible and credible, but useful.

Like black feminist cultural production proliferating since the late nineteenth century, Ida's return to American lynching culture in "Saving White Face" performs specific conventions and strategies which have heretofore been misunderstood. Ida's character represents the ways black women have "reconstructed womanhood" in the face of white supremacist discursive and material practice. As noted by Hazel Carby, "the turn of the century . . . was one of intense productivity for Afro-American women," through works of both fiction and non-fiction. Examinations of these works abounds, especially regarding the ways they analyzed and created new images of black womanhood "not as passive representations of history but as active influence within history."[98] Ida performs as an active influence within the play, representing "a particular analysis of the position of the black woman that effectively challenged the terms of contemporary debate about gender and about race."[99]

As aforementioned, excerpts of Gwendolyn Brooks' poem, "A Bronzeville Mother Loiters in Mississippi. Meanwhile, a Mississippi Mother Burns Bacon" functioned in multiple ways in "Saving White Face." Brooks' poem serves as one "counterpoint to the rhythm created by the dialogue"[100] and was recited while accompanied by stylized movement that was repeated throughout the production. In an opening scene, before any of the adapted dialogue begins, Lily Cox joins the narrator, Ida, at center stage where together they stylistically moved as if applying makeup while reciting,

Ida: From the first it had been like a Ballad.
         It had the beat inevitable. It had the blood.
Lily: Herself: the milk white maid, the "maid mild"
         Of the ballad.

The opening text of Brooks' poem presents "the lynching story" as a positivist narrative in which Lily performs as an object of the narrative as opposed to a subject. Brooks frames the lynching story as a ballad, which reflects a Romantic, or idealized, narrative. As the drama progresses, Lily's position within the lynching performance is foregrounded, especially with regard to her willingness to "play along" or comply with the lynching performances despite the numerous injustices she takes part in and witnesses, as well as the ways she suffers despite "the lynching story's" claims. Lily's performance as white woman subject in anti-lynching plays is examined more fully in the following chapter.

"Saving White Face" uses a black feminist performance-based convention of rejecting white women as "a universal measure for womanhood at large"[101] as well as holding white women performers accountable for their complicity in lynching. "Saving White Face" accomplishes this by staging a "simultaneity" which it "borrows . . . from drama for the purpose of vivifying and clarifying narrative action"[102] to foreground a split subjectivity of its modern characters, especially Lily Cox. As this passage shows, "Saving White Face" performs simultaneity when either Ida and Lily or Lily and Floyd Cox recite the same lines at the same time. In doing so, "Saving White Face" depicts Lily's split subjectivity while performing as a woman as well as simultaneously performing as a white racist. In part, Lily's split subjectivity is noteworthy because she is presented as an intersectional subject in the same way as Ida. Molly Littlewood McKibbin evidences this idea through her close reading of Brooks' poem in her article "Southern Patriarchy and the Figure of the White Woman in 'A Bronzeville Mother,'" in which McKibbin compares several of Brooks' poems to conclude

> Her poems about school and housing integration and interracial sex help explain the ordinariness of racial violence (and thus how the white woman in "A Bronzeville Mother" might have come to expect lynching), but also how the suffering of African Americans is so widespread and apparent that the white woman should have known better.[103]

Finally, Brooks' poem foregrounds a critique of white women repetitively lodged by the earliest black feminists that can be referenced in the following section of the Combahee River Collective's statement:

> As Black feminists we are made constantly and painfully aware of how little effort white women have made to understand and combat their racism, which requires among other things that they have a more superficial comprehension of race, color and Black history and culture.[104]

Psychoanalyzing "the lynching story"

Through Gwendolyn Brooks' poetry, "Saving White Face" depicts a psychoanalysis of the lynching story.

IDA: That boy must have been surprised! For These were grown ups. Grown ups were supposed to be wise. And the Fine

Prince – and that other – so tall, so broad, So Grown! Perhaps
the boy had never guessed That the trouble with grown ups
was that under the magnificent shell of adulthood, just under,
Waited the baby full of tantrums

Brooks here refers to lynching as a performance of whiteness
immaturity. Instead of (psychologically) mature adults, the young
(black) lynching victim encounters behavior usually exhibited by a
toddler, "a baby full of tantrums." Ida remarks on the surprise of the
young black boy who was subjected to childlike behavior of others who were older than he. As black feminist narrator character,
Ida performs psychoanalysis of whiteness through the text of Brooks'
poem, which functions as an "alternative medium" within the play
providing a "counterpoint to the rhythm created by the dialogue."[105]

In *Mourning and Modernity: Essays in the Psychoanalysis of Contemporary Society*, Isaac Balbus draws on Melanie Klein's psychoanalytic
theory to explain Jim Crow segregation and racism. Melanie Klein,
initially a protégé of Sigmund Freud, was a foremost member of
the "object relations" school of psychoanalysis, "whose proponents
argued that the basic human striving is for relationships, rather than
mere gratification of primitive drives."[106] Kleinian psychoanalysis
outlines an individual's psychological development as a process in
which, as an infant, an individual passes through a "paranoid-schizoid" stage. This position is a manifestation of an "infant's cognitive
immaturity"[107] and one in which the infant cannot reconcile simultaneous feelings of gratification and frustration that it feels towards
its mother, specifically her breast. Consequently, the infant experiences a radical split in reality between "a benevolent, all-good breast
and the fantasy of a malevolent, all-bad breast."[108] These feelings
precipitate feelings of overwhelming love as well as destructive fury.
Later, around the end of its first year, the child "develops the cognitive capacity to recognize that the good and bad mothers are in fact
one in the same";[109] nevertheless, the child experiences a "depressive
guilt" for the intense anger it once felt. Ideally, the child overcomes
these feelings to become a "depressively integrated individual," who
is "prepared for relationships with self and others that are based on
a realistic appreciation of the inevitability of ambivalence within
those relationships."[110] However, integration is not automatic; if it
is not achieved, the child's arrested development manifests as either
an over-idealization of the mother in an attempt to ward off its guilt,
or demonization of its mother as a way of denying its need for her.

Social and political theorist Isaac Balbus extends upon Klein's analysis to indicate that Western childrearing practices as practiced in American society "militate against depressive integration at the oral, anal, and genital stages of individual development";[111] therefore concluding, "Defensive splitting on the part of individuals is pervasive." Furthermore, Balbus goes on to explain, "white racism is fueled by the primitive passions of the paranoid-schizoid position and that it discourages people from transcending that position."[112] According to Balbus, American society, fueled by racism, thwarts the maturity of all of its citizens.

"The lynching story," as white supremacist narrative, can now be read through Balbus' psychoanalytic lens to discuss how each subject, including the exiled black woman, ends up lynched. If we read "the lynching story" using Balbus' framework, lynching can be understood as an ultimate "discouragement" against transcendence of the paranoid schizoid position. In general, the whiteness performance practice prevents its subjects from maturing as psychologically, physically, socially and culturally. Specifically, the narrative freezes each subject into an immature state that he/she must maintain thereby reproducing white supremacy. Even further, "the lynching story" is supported by other (interdisciplinary) cultural narratives that reinforce it, as well as institutionalized cultural practices materializing the immature subject position.

"Saving White Face" functions as a critical examination of "the lynching story" by staging the cultural narrative in order to effectively clarify its nature and performance. In much the same way that a lawyer visually depicts sworn testimony or a crime's sequence of events, lynching plays depict versions of "the lynching story," especially those that have already been actually executed, albeit in secret. Not only do lynching plays examine "the lynching story," but they also examine other intersectional whiteness narratives (myth-rituals) reproduced by lynching such as segregation, consumerism and the black "brute."

Staging Jim Crow segregation and whiteface masking in "Saving White Face"

"Saving White Face's" staging, like Western cultural binaries spatially (re)produced by "the lynching story" and Jim Crow segregation, splits into two realms: a "domestic" space that serves as a kitchen/restaurant area, as well as a "work" space that converts from a pool hall into a newspaper office. The scenes' blocking make "Ida's" movements efficient; she performs between both sides as a Chamber Theatre "narrator-character," also "doubling" as the drama's two white male patriarchs. In order to mark her "double" performance, Ida dons a white, Lone Ranger style mask when performing as white men. This white mask makes literal "the masking function of the rape charge in lynching" since, as Wells-Barnett first noted, "less than 29 percent of all lynching even involved the charge of rape."[113] By marking Ida's dual portrayal of Floyd Cox and Clayton Pinochet's father with a white Lone ranger style mask, "Saving White Face" effectively layered conventions to affect the mood of the production which created an excess structure of feeling within the performance. By adding this cheap prop, the play is saturated with an uneasy sense, making it hard for those who watched it to feel unaffected by it. Paradoxically, by putting the mask on Ida as she played these white men, an unveiling occurred. Ida's white mask inverts whiteface masking as performed within lynching performances (through the use of a Ku Klux Klan hood or not) to mark the violence, exploitation and miscarriages of justice that perpetuate white supremacy with no accountability. Ida's performance of double-ness can also be thought to represent a blurring of "the lynching story's" binary race and gender constructions, as well as those between the "public" crime of lynching and the "private" crime of rape, a point *Southern Horrors* also makes.[114]

More pointedly, "Saving White Face's" staging echoes Jim Crow segregation. According to Grace Elizabeth Hale in *Making Whiteness: The Culture of Segregation in the South 1890–1940*, segregation was a principle means through which Southern whites "made a new collective white identity across lines of gender and class and a new racial distinctiveness."[115] Southern whites instituted segregation as a spatial method of social control through which whites "made modern racial meaning not just by creating boundaries but also by crossing them,"[116] especially with regard to donning blackface but also including practices up to and including disrupting and intruding in black households. Hale traces the performance-based, spatial practice of segregation to an 1866 narrative written by Edward Alfred Pollard, a journalist from Richmond, Virginia, that reconfigured "national conflict from sectional to racial war."[117] White Southerners went on to craft other Reconstruction era fiction and "nonfiction" that divided their narrative antagonists into binary categories such as "loyal" versus "betraying free darkies," as well as "niggers" and

"Yankees." However, it was Thomas Dixon, a North Carolina born novelist, who "transformed more completely than other white writers the complex of class, race and sectional alliances and conflicts of the Reconstruction era into Pollard's race war" in *The Leopard's Spots* and *The Clansman*.[118]

From Ida B. Wells-Barnett to "Ida"

Like the anti-lynching/rape activism of her namesake, Ida B. Wells-Barnett (1862–1931), "Ida's" role as narrator-character in "Saving White Face" proves pivotal. Wells-Barnett's pamphlet *Southern Horrors: Lynch Law in All Its Phases* (1892), identified as "a point of origin in American critical thought on lynching,"[119] directly confronted "the lynching story's" complex of race and gender constructions by re-reading discursive practices in and around lynching, providing an alternative way of understanding the practice, thereby chartering "new ideological territory."[120]

Journalistically, Wells-Barnett visibly interrogated "the lynching story" by reprinting accounts of lynchings as they appeared in newspapers and marking them up with "unorthodox punctuation." Schechter points out, "By disrupting these texts with quotation and question marks, Wells-Barnett mocked their authority and created space for her own findings and re-readings of the material."[121] Ida B. Wells-Barnett performs as one of the first black feminist cultural critics of the modern era. She effectively contests "the lynching story" while is being hardened into an excuse for lynching that was so commonly used, it was referred to as "the usual crime."

Even further, Wells-Barnett's interrogation of "the lynching story" can also be understood as early cultural analysis of the practice testing not only the narrative's veracity, but its sanity, as well. Wells-Barnett effectively marks "the lynching story" as source material for cultural analysis of white supremacist cultural production emerging during a post-Reconstruction era. Her identification of lynching as a discursive and material practice which, like all human culture, can be examined structurally reflects her early criticism of white supremacy which lynchers mischaracterized as a "necessary evil" performed in defense of white womanhood against the "brute passion of the Negro." Wells-Barnett's analysis counteracts gas lighting manipulation and positivist-based claims that whiteness operates outside the realm of time and space.

Wells-Barnett points out the psychological projection as well as

> how the miscegenation laws of the South only operate against
> the legitimate union of the races; they leave the white man free
> to seduce all the colored girls he can, but it is death to the colored
> man who yields to the force and advances of a similar attraction
> in white women.[122]

At the end of Chapter 2 of *Southern Horrors*, Wells-Barnett cites
several cases in which black girl children were raped by white men
who were never subjected to brutal lynchings, even when the child
sustained injuries for life or died due to the assaults.[123] Wells-Barnett
effectively proves an inconsistency by white men who claim to carry
out lynching to protect defenseless women.

In much the same way as her namesake, "Ida" performs black feminist performance strategies in "Saving White Face," including *occu-
pying* "the lynching story," performance in a blues aesthetic, as well
as "mirroring" Lily, the white (modern) woman subject of the play.

Black feminist performance strategies in "Saving White Face"

"Ida" opens "Saving White Face" by directly addressing the audience,
not only creating *mise en scène*, but reminding the audience of their
tie to the (social) drama:

> (Ida enters stage right under spotlight and stands behind a
> table that it downstage left where she seems to be preparing
> food. She is wearing an apron, holding a rolling pin and
> a shotgun. Behind her reads, "The Busy Bee Café." She is
> muttering to herself about lynching, injustice, murdering
> children. She seems almost crazy. She sees a fly and begins
> to trail it around the right side of the stage. She threatens it
> and the audience several times with the rolling pin and shot
> gun. She seems to lose track of the fly and returns to cook-
> ing (maybe rolling dough with the rolling pin). (She sees the
> fly again. She crashes the rolling pin onto the table, killing
> the fly.)

Ida: I told that fly, Your day is coming. Yessir. (She looks directly at
the audience.) Don't you think your day ain't coming.

"Ida" directly confronts the audience as (prospective) perpetuators of "the lynching story," reminding them that they are subject to natural laws that would hold them accountable. According to D. Soyini Madison, "Ida" performs an embodied framing[124] of the play, heightening the mood of "Saving White Face" to set up its interpretive frame as black feminist performance. Ida's non-normative return[125] to "the lynching story" in "Saving White Face" constitutes a (black) feminist strategy in which the narrator is situated "as an *occupation* (emphasis in original) into which various performers are hailed."[126] As opposed to an omniscient narrator position, "Ida's" *occupation* of "the lynching story" as "narrator-character" "performs a function and is authorized as an expert based on the power and control that the role itself commands" which "undercut(s) the emphasis on the authority of the Individual, while exposing the interpellative method by which certain subjects are hailed into power." It also "expose(s) the fundamental, if devoutly obscured, vulnerability of any particular individual who wields power, suggesting that power must be maintained through the same performative functions – citationality, repetition and naming – that condition identity formation."[127] Furthermore, "Ida's" black feminist *occupation* of "the lynching story" not only renders her visible in lynching culture, but presents black women as "full historical subjects"[128] as well. Unlike her aforementioned exiled position from "the lynching story," black women's performance in lynching culture is not based nor privileged upon her race, class or gender, since as narrator-character, she "functions as a dialectic with access to knowledge of the insider/outsider, southerner/northerner, victim/survivor."[129] Both offstage and onstage, Ida B. Wells-Barnett and "Saving White Face's" "Ida," "embrace(s) liminality and gain(s) richer, if less stable ideological terrain from which to work."[130]

"Ida's" role in "Saving White Face," most significantly, marks Wells-Barnett's black feminist anti-lynching activism by making material what Wells-Barnett performed discursively: a return of black women to lynching culture. Specifically, it was Wells-Barnett who first

> made black women visible in the dynamics of southern lynching and sexualized racism. Wells documented not only black women's sideline suffering but attacks-lynching and rapes on black women and girls. . . . She stressed the general public's ignorance of black women's experiences . . . for which nobody is lynched and no notice is taken.[131]

However, instead of inspiring widespread accolades, Wells-Barnett's anti-lynching efforts incited racists who "wrecked her press office."[132] Also, since her critiques "destabilized gender dualisms and racial hierarchies and thereby threatened the very terms by which power, order and legitimacy were understood by many middle-class Americans, black or white, clubwomen or clergy"[133], Wells-Barnett's activism caused gender anxiety, fueling repression. Unable to recognize her cutting edge efforts, Wells-Barnett's anti-lynching/rape activism did not get the contemporary recognition it deserved. American racism and sexism intersected, marginalizing her voice though she ceaselessly raised it as a leading black feminist educator, journalist, suffragist and human rights advocate.[134] Finally, Ida's *occupation* of "the lynching story" is one way that "Saving White Face" reflects a black feminist Chamber Theatre method. In much the same way that Diekmann "refunctions" Chamber Theatre conventions, "Saving White Face" repurposes "the use of narrator,"[135] "alienation,"[136] split subjectivity,"[137] "the use of the mirror"[138] and "the relationship between Adapter and Adaptation"[139] to represent a black feminist method. Black feminism is critical to Chamber Theatre method because of the ways it interrogates the method as a whiteness performance practice. In addition to reimagining Chamber Theatre conventions (as outlined throughout this chapter), "Saving White Face" performs in a blues(woman) aesthetic, another black feminist representational mode marking black women's return to "the lynching story."

"Ida" as blueswoman performer

"Ida's" *occupation* of "the lynching story" evokes another black feminism, a blueswoman aesthetic. "Saving White Face's" blues aesthetic directly references Campbell's novel title, *Your Blues Ain't Like Mine*. Additionally, Brooks' poetry performs a blues "counterpoint to the rhythm"[140] created by Campbell's text. "Saving White Face's" blues fulfills Stephens' second criteria of an "aesthetic tradition" that comprises an "essential element of the drama."[141] Within "Saving White Face's" lynching culture, "Ida" performs as blueswoman, setting up "an alternative form of representation, an oral and musical woman's culture that explicitly addresses the contradictions of feminism, sexuality and power."[142] Angela Y. Davis' groundbreaking treatise, *Blues Legacies and Black Feminism* (1998), analyzes historical blueswomen songs as black feminist archives. Blueswomen oral tradition reflects "the genius with which former slaves forged new traditions that simultaneously contested the slave past and preserved some of the rich cultural products of slavery."[143] Blueswomen shouted out about "the new troubles black people faced in a world that still refused to accept them as equals, a society that thrived on the systematic exploitation and discrimination meted out to the former slaves."[144] "Saving White Face" invokes a black, blueswomen tradition musically traced to Gertrude "Ma" Rainey, Bessie Smith and Billie Holiday and extended upon by Alberta Hunter, Ethel Waters and others.[145] Hazel Carby cogently identifies the (song of) blueswomen not only as "central mechanism(s) of cultural mediation" but the primary means of expression of the disrupted social relations associated with urban migration."[146] In performances of "Saving White Face" since 2008, "Ida's" blues aesthetics mediates the election of Barack Hussein Obama, the United States of America's first black president.

Through "Ida," "Saving White Face" foregrounds black women's storytelling tradition, also known as Testifyin'.[147] Like a blueswoman singer who simultaneously preserves tradition, "shouts out" about injustice and mediates cultural change, Ida (re)tells the plot's lynching event thereby exhibiting Judith Stephens' third criteria of lynching drama, "a woman's telling of events."[148] Shortly after the lynching has occurred in "Saving White Face," Ida reports:

IDA: By Saturday afternoon, the colored section of Hopewell was shrouded in fear, anger and confusion. Every colored person in town had learned that Armstrong Todd was killed by the Coxes because he spoke French to Lily Cox. They also understood that he'd been murdered because of the Supreme Court's ruling against segregated schools.

Carby's theoretical framework of blues(woman) discourse as "empowered presence"[149] also helps to illuminate Ida's blueswoman role/function. Ida not only "reports" the news of the lynching, she also expresses "black truth" or a counter hegemonic logic expressed among blacks, a part of "the lynching story" left out of the original version. Consequently, "Ida's" blues functions not only as a medium through which change is negotiated, but performs as immaterial labor, or "labor that produces an immaterial good, such as a service, knowledge or communication."[150] Specifically, "Ida's" blues functions as affective labor, "the binding element"[151] of immaterial labor whose "products are intangible: a feeling of ease, well-being, satisfaction,

excitement, passion – even a sense of connectedness or community. . . . What affective labor produces are social networks, forms of
community, biopower."[152] Inasmuch as affective labor is associated
with "gendered labor," or women's work, it is subject to subordination and domination. Even worse, these effects are compounded
when blueswoman performance is produced by black women whose
work is always already vulnerable to these assaults. As discussed by
Schechter, for example, Ida B. Wells-Barnett's anti-lynching activism was effectively subordinated and dominated by male and white
women led efforts.[153] However, this tendency is reversed in "Saving
White Face" since "Ida's" labor as narrator-character is never sub-
sumed under anyone else's. One way "Ida's" blueswoman performance proves equal to other subjects is by mirroring Lily Cox. By
mirroring Lily Cox, Ida performs both sameness and difference to
make Lily accountable for her role in the lynching story, re-position-
ing her from an object to a subject position.

Notes

1 *Safe* was staged as one of three one-act plays performed in a showcase of Black
   Drama and HBCU performance. The other plays that were staged were *Sacrifice*
   by Thelma Myrtle Duncan as well as *The House of Sham* by Willis Richardson
   retrieved from Willis Richardson and May Miller, *Negro History in Thirteen
   Plays* (Washington, DC: The Associated Publishers, 1935).
2 The Digital Library of Georgia, University of Georgia Libraries, "The Blues,
   Black Vaudeville and the Silver Screen: Selections from the Records of Macon's
   Douglass Theatre," (2005). http://dlg.galileo.usg.edu/douglass/index.php.
   Accessed May 21, 2019.
3 Ibid.
4 Glover's clothes were cut to shreds and sold as souvenirs subsequent to his
   murder.
5 It is reported that police arrived just in time to prevent lynchers from setting
   Glover's body on fire, and with it, the Douglass Theatre.
6 Fuoss extensively discusses the prominent figuration of "display of performance
   traces" as a subsequent lynching performance.
7 Ibid.
8 Michelle Hiskey, "Pilgrims Bear Witness to Racial Reconciliation at Georgia Lynching Site," (October 25, 2016). www.episcopalchurch.org. Accessed
   May 21, 2019.
9 Ibid.
10 The lynching of Sam Hose is fully reviewed in Chapter 3 of this book in which
   I conduct a close reading of Georgia Douglass Johnson's anti-lynching play *Safe*
   (c. 1929) as performed on the campus of Fort Valley State University (FVSU)
   as part of a lynching play series. FVSU is a Historically Black College and University (HBCU) in Fort Valley, Georgia.
11 Angela Y. Davis, *Blues Legacies and Black Feminisms: "Ma Rainey," Bessie Smith
   and Billie Holiday* (New York, NY: Vintage Books, 1998), XV.

12 Victor Turner, *From Ritual to Theatre: The Human Seriousness of Play* (New York, NY: PAJ Publications, 1982), 27.

13 In Southern, *The Music of Black Americans*, 331.

14 I employ Jane Blocker's discussion of using performance and performativity as a framework for "performativity, identity and exile," as found in the "Introduction" to *Where Is Ana Mendieta?* 23–27.

15 Davis, *Blues Legacies and Black Feminisms*, XV.

16 Peggy Phelan, *Unmarked: The Politics of Performance* (London: Routledge, 1993), 5.

17 See Elizabeth Grace Hale's *Making Whiteness: The Culture of Segregation in the South, 1890–1940* (New York, NY: Vintage Books, 1998).

18 Perkins and Stephens, *Strange Fruit*, 7.

19 Phelan, *Unmarked*, 3.

20 Monumental time applies to an overall conception of black feminist performance traditions as well as the anti-lynching drama tradition as an individual tradition as illustrated through Grimke's work as well as FVSU's lynching play series which is documented in Chapter 3.

21 Wilmer, S. E., "Restaging the Nation: The Work of Suzan-Lori Parks," *Modern Drama* 43, no. 3 (Fall 2000), 447.

22 Haley, *No Mercy Here*, 4.

23 Lisa A. Anderson, *Black Feminisms in Contemporary Drama* (Urbana, IL: University of Illinois Press, 2011), 4.

24 Perkins foregrounds black women's interdisciplinary contributions in her introductory essay titled, "The Impact on the Art of African American Women," in *Strange Fruit* (1998).

25 Koritha Mitchell, *Living With Lynching: African American Lynching Plays, Performance and Citizenship 1890–1930* (Chicago, IL: University of Illinois Press, 2011), 45.

26 Ibid, 211.

27 Here I refer to Alain Locke's statement regarding the preservation of folklore in black drama as referred to by Elin Diamond, "Folk Modernism: Zora Neale Hurston's Gestural Drama," *Modern Drama* 58, no. 1 (Spring 2015), 112.

28 See Mitchell's *Living With Lynching*.

29 See Lindsey's *Colored No More* (2017).

30 Ibid, 113.

31 Blocker, *Where Is Ana Mendieta?* 25.

32 Lindsey, *Colored No More*, 113.

33 Jimoh, "Mapping the Terrain of Black Writing," 489.

34 Refers to the post-slavery term as well as the black feminist cultural criticism performed by Hazel Carby in *Reconstructing Womanhood: The Emergence of the Afro-American Woman Novelist* (New York, NY: Oxford University Press, 1987); and Ericka M. Miller, *The Other Reconstruction: Where Violence and Womanhood Meet in the Writings of Ida B. Wells-Barnett, Angelina Weld Grimke and Nella Larsen* (New York, NY: Garland Publishing, Inc., 2000).

35 See Crystal N. Feimster's chapter, "The Lynching of Black and White Women," in *Southern Horrors: Women and the Politics of Rape and Lynching* (Cambridge, MA: Harvard University Press, 2009).

36 Miller, *The Other Reconstruction*, 58.

37 Ibid, 86.

38 Mitchell reviews Grimke's revisions in the "Rachel and Revision" section of *Living With Lynching*. I include revision as a form of repetition as a black feminist performance strategy used by anti-lynching dramatists.
39 Daylanne K. English discusses anti-lynching drama in both her essay *Unnatural Selections: Eugenics in American Modernism and Harlem Renaissance* (Chapel Hill, NC: University of North Carolina Press, 2004), as well as her book *Each Hour Redeem: Time and Justice in African American Literature* (2013).
40 English, *Unnatural Selections*, 95.
41 W.E.B. Du Bois, "Criteria in Negro Art," *The Crisis* 32 (1926), 290–97.
42 Ibid.
43 Kirschke, "Art in Crisis," 52.
44 Mitchell, "Living with Lynching," 10.
45 Ndounou, "Drama for Neglected People."
46 Brittney C. Cooper, *Beyond Respectability: The Intellectual Thought of Race Women* (Urbana, IL: University of Illinois Press, 2017), 15.
47 Ibid, 29.
48 Ibid.
49 Ibid.
50 Ibid, 32.
51 Fuoss, "Lynching Performances," 5.
52 Carby, *Reconstructing Womanhood*, 95.
53 Haley, *No Mercy Here*, 6.
54 See Feimster, *Southern Horrors*, in which she narrates a historical account of the anti-rape activism of Rebecca Latimer Felton who after first advocating against rape on behalf of both white and black women, ceased to represent black women in order to advocate solely for their own "public role and . . . political power." (126).
55 Mitchell, *Living With Lynching*, 62.
56 Ericka M. Miller identifies refusal as a black feminist performance strategy in Grimke's short story, "The Closing Door." Haley also theorizes "sabotage and radical black feminist refusal" as strategies employed by black women who were imprisoned for having disrupted local structures that exploited, imprisoned and raped them. I borrow Haley's conception here and apply it to Rachel in order to fully articulate Rachel's refusal of John Strong's hand in marriage. Haley's articulation fully fleshes out black feminist sabotage and refusal among imprisoned black women as well as the blueswomen who represented their struggles through song.
57 Haley, *No Mercy Here*, 6.
58 Ibid.
59 See. Josephine Lee, "Teaching 'A Doll's House,' 'Rachel' and 'Marisol:' Domestic Ideals, Possessive Individuals and Modern Drama," *Modern Drama* 50, no. 4 (2007), 620–37. Like Ibsen's *A Doll's House*, Rachel is based on a three act structure and depicts a young (white) woman's coming to consciousness with respect to marriage and family.
60 I refer to Anna Julia Cooper's 1899 newspaper article entitled, "Colored Women as Wage Earners" as discussed in Vivian May's "Writing the Self Into Being: Anna Julia Cooper's Textual Politics," *African American Review* 43, no. 1 (Spring 2009), 17–34.
61 Stephens and Perkins, *Strange Fruit*.

62 Ibid, 10.

63 Ibid, 9.

64 See Nikki M. Taylor, *Driven Toward Madness: The Fugitive Slave Margaret Garner and the Tragedy on the Ohio* (Athens, OH: University of Ohio Press, 2016).

65 Miller, *The Other Reconstruction*, 75.

66 Ibid, 54.

67 Ibid.

68 Rachel's rebuttals echo Anna Julia Cooper's rhetorical strategies as identified by Vivian May in "Writing the Self Into Being."

69 David Krasner, *History of Modern Drama* (Hoboken, NJ: Wiley, 2011), 8.

70 Ibid, 9.

71 Ibid, 10.

72 Ibid, 6.

73 Mary Church Terrell, "Lynching from a Negro's Point of View," *The North American Review* 178, no. 571 (June 1904), 865.

74 In Under Lynching's Shadow: Grimke's Call for Domestic Reconfiguration in *Rachel*, Anne Mai Yee Jansen refers to Rachel's decision to forego having children as a choice to "mother the unborn" which is a non-normative choice effectively reconfiguring the black family.

75 Hale, *Making Whiteness*, 105.

76 Haley, *No Mercy Here*, 5.

77 Ibid, 106.

78 Simon Bennett, "The Fragmented Self, the Reproduction of the Self, and Reproduction in Beckett and in the Theater of the Absurd," in Joseph H. Smith (ed.), *The World of Samuel Beckett* (Baltimore, MD: Johns Hopkins University, 1991), 163; quoted in Claudia Barnett, "A Prison of Object Relations: Adrienne Kennedy's 'Funnyhouse of a Negro'," *Modern Drama* 40, no. 3 (Fall 1997), 374 (11).

79 Krasner, *History of Modern Drama*, 18.

80 Blocker's discussion of performance and performativity in *Where Is Ana Mendieta?* informs this part of the discussion.

81 Ibid.

82 *Rachel* is well known to have been the first black play produced for a popular audience, but it should also be noted that Willis Richardson reported being inspired to write plays based on seeing the first production of *Rachel* as discussed by Lindsey in *Colored No More* (2017).

83 Miller, *The Other Reconstruction*, XXI.

84 Lisa M. Anderson, *Black Feminism in Contemporary Drama* (Urbana, IL: University of Illinois Press, 2008), 115.

85 Lara E. Dieckmann, "Toward a Feminist Chamber Theatre Method," *Text and Performance Quarterly* 19 (1999), 38.

86 Schechter, "Unsettled Business," 292.

87 Although she doesn't explicitly reference "the lynching story," Sarah Haley references other intersecting narratives through which black women were imprisoned and exploited in *No Mercy Here* (2016).

88 "Saving White Face" depicts two precipitating instances of domestic violence: one between Lily and Floyd and the other between Clayton Pinochet and his father. "Saving White Face," as anti-lynching activism, blurs a binary between white "public" and "private" terrorism.

89 Fuoss, "Lynching Performances," 9.
90 Raper, *The Tragedy of Lynching*, 481; Trelease, *White Terror*, quotes in McGovern, *Anatomy of a Lynching*, 2.
91 *Birth of a Nation* was adapted and directed by D. W. Griffith and released on February 8, 1915.
92 Gunning, *Race, Rape and Lynching*, 6.
93 Ibid, 22.
94 See Elizabeth Alexander's *The New Jim Crow: Mass Incarceration in the Age of Colorblindness* (New York, NY: The New Press, 2012).
95 I borrow this term from Vivian May's analysis of Anna Julia Cooper's oeuvre in "Writing the Self Into Being," 19.
96 Blocker, *Where Is Ana Mendieta?* 24.
97 Wilmer, "Restaging the Nation," 444.
98 Carby, *Reconstructing Womanhood*, 95.
99 Ibid, 97.
100 This feature is one of the characteristics of lynching plays as identified by Judith L. Stephens in *Strange Fruit*.
101 May, "Writing the Self Into Being," 25.
102 Robert S. Breen, *Chamber Theatre* (Englewood Cliffs, NJ: Prentice-Hall, 1978), 4.
103 Molly Littlewood McKibbin, "Southern Patriarchy and the Figure of the White Woman in Gwendolyn Brooks' 'A Bronzeville Mother Loiters in Mississippi: Meanwhile, a Mississippi Mother Burns Bacon'," *African American Review* 44, no. 4 (2011), 667–85. *Project MUSE*, muse.jhu.edu/article/484907.
104 "Combahee River Collective," in Barbara Smith (ed.), *Home Girls: A Black Feminist Anthology* (New Brunswick, NJ: Rutgers University Press, 2000), 273.
105 Perkins and Stephens, *Strange Fruit*, 10.
106 Stephen Gladwell, "Melanie Klein: From Theory to Reality," *The Lancet* 340, no. 8828 (November 7, 1992), 1149 (1).
107 Isaac Balbus, "The Psychodynamics of Racial Reparations," in *Mourning and Modernity* (New York, NY: Other Press, 2005), 94.
108 Ibid, 95.
109 Ibid.
110 Ibid, 97.
111 Ibid, 99.
112 Ibid.
113 Schechter, "Unsettled Business," 295.
114 Ibid, 301.
115 Hale, *Making Whiteness*, 9.
116 Ibid, 8.
117 Ibid, 76.
118 Ibid, 73.
119 Schechter, "Unsettled, Business," 293.
120 Ibid, 301.
121 Ibid, 293.
122 Jones Royster, *Southern Horrors and Other Writings*, 58–59.
123 Ibid.

124 D. Soyini Madison, "That Was My Occupation: Oral Narrative, Performance and Black Feminist Thought," *Text and Performance Quarterly* 13, no. 3 (July 1993), 229.

125 It should be noted here that Wells-Barnett actually adopted the moniker "exile" as part of her activism.

126 Dieckmann, "Toward a Feminist Chamber," 45.

127 Ibid.

128 Schechter, "Unsettled, Business," 301.

129 Ibid, 304.

130 Ibid.

131 quoted in Ibid, 296–97.

132 Ibid, 304.

133 Ibid, 308.

134 See Paula Giddings, *Ida: A Sword Among Lions: Ida B. Wells and the Campaign Against Lynching* (New York, NY: Amistad Press, 2008).

135 Dieckmann, "Toward a Feminist Chamber," 43.

136 Ibid, 45.

137 Ibid, 47.

138 Ibid, 49.

139 Ibid, 51.

140 Perkins and Stephens, *Strange Fruit*, 10.

141 Ibid.

142 Hazel V. Carby *Cultures in Babylon: Black Britain and African America* (London: Verso, 1999), 10.

143 Davis, *Blues Legacies and Black Feminism*, XIX.

144 Ibid, 224.

145 For further discussion of these women's contribution, see Hazel Carby, "Women, Migration and the Formation of Blues Culture," in *Cultures in Babylon*, 7–63.

146 Ibid, 36.

147 Ibid, 11.

148 Perkins and Stephens, *Strange Fruit*, 10–11.

149 Carby, *Cultures in Babylon*, 8.

150 Michael Hardt. 1999. "Affective Labor." *Boundary* 2 26 (2), 94.

151 Ibid, 95.

152 Ibid, 96.

153 See Schechter's, "Unsettled Business."

Bibliography

Anderson, Lisa M. 2008. *Black Feminism in Contemporary Drama*. Urbana, IL: University of Illinois Press.

Balbus, Isaac. 2005. *Mourning and Modernity: Essays in the Psychoanalysis of Contemporary Society*. New York, NY: Other Press.

Barnett, Claudia. 1997. "A Prison of Object Relations: Adrienne Kennedy's 'Funnyhouse of a Negro'." *Modern Drama* 40, no. 3: 374–84.

Bauman, Richard. 1977. *Verbal Art as Performance*. Prospect Heights, IL: Waveland Press.

Blocker, Jane. 1999. *Where Is Ana Mendieta: Identity, Performance and Exile.* Durham, NC: Duke University Press.

Carby, Hazel. 1987. *Reconstructing Womanhood: The Emergence of the Afro-American Woman Novelist.* Oxford: Oxford University Press.

Carlson, Marvin. 1996. *Performance: A Critical Introduction.* London: Routledge.

Cooper, Brittney C. 2017. *Beyond Respectability.* Urbana, IL: University of Illinois Press.

Davis, Angela. 1998. *Blues Legacies and Black Feminism.* New York, NY: Vintage Books.

Diamond, Elin. 2015. "Folk Modernism, Zora Neale Hurston's Gestural Drama." *Modern Drama* 58, no. 1: 112–34.

The Digital Library of Georgia, University of Georgia Libraries. 2005. "The Blues, Black Vaudeville and the Silver Screen: Selections from the Records of Macon's Douglass Theatre." Accessed May 21, 2019. http://dlg.galileo.usg.edu/douglass/index.php.

Dieckmann, Lara E. 1999. "Towards a Feminist Chamber Theatre Method." *Text and Performance Quarterly* 19: 38–56.

Du Bois, W.E.B. 1926. "Criteria of Negro Art." *The Crisis* 32: 290–97.

English, Daylanne. 2004. *Blessed Are the Barren: Lynching, Reproduction, and the Drama of New Negro Womanhood, 1916–1930.* Chapel Hill, NC: University of North Carolina Press.

———. 2013. *Each Hour Redeem: Time and Justice in American Literature.* Minneapolis, MN: University of Minnesota Press.

Feimster, Nicole. 2009. *Southern Horrors: Women and Politics of Rape and Lynching.* Cambridge, MA: Harvard University Press.

Finnegan, Cara A., A. Susan Owen, and Ehrenhaus Peter. 2011. "Review Essay: Looking at Lynching: Spectacle Resistance and Contemporary Transformations." *Quarterly Journal of Speech*: 100–13.

Fuoss, Kirk. 1999. "Lynching Performances, Theatres of Violence." *Text and Performance Quarterly*: 1–37.

Giddings, Paula. 2008. *Ida: A Sword Among Lions: Ida B. Wells and the Campaign Against Lynching.* New York, NY: Amistad Press.

Gladwell, Stephen. 1992. "Melanie Klein: From Theory to Reality." *The Lancet*: 1149.

Gunning, Sandra. 1996. *Race, Rape and Lynching: The Red Record of American Literature 1890–1912.* New York, NY: Oxford University Press.

Hale, Elizabeth Grace. 1998. *Making Whiteness: The Culture of Segregation in the South 1890–1940.* New York, NY: Vintage Books.

Haley, Sarah. 2016. *No Mercy Here: Gender, Punishment and Making of Jim Crow Modernity.* Chapel Hill, NC: University of North Carolina Press.

Harris, Trudier. 1984. *Exorcising Blackness: Historical and Literary Lynching and Burning Rituals.* Bloomington, IN: Indiana University Press.

Hiskey, Michelle. 2016. "Pilgrims Bear Witness to Racial Reconciliation at Georgia Lynching Site." October 25. Accessed May 21, 2019. www.episcopalchurch.org/posts/socialjusticeandadvocacy/pilgrims-bear-witness-racial-reconciliation-georgia-lynching-site.

Hoelscher, Steven. 2003. "Making Place, Making Race: Performances of Whiteness in the Jim Crow South." *Annals of the Association of American Geographers* 93, no. 3: 657–86.

Jansen, Anne Mai Yee. 2014. "Under Lynching's Shadow: Grimke's Call for Domestic Reconfiguration in 'Rachel'." *African American Review*: 391–402.

Kelley, Robin D. G. 2002. "This Battlefield Called Life: Black Feminist Dreams." In *Freedom Dreams: The Radical Black Imagination*, 135–56. Boston, MA: Beacon Press.

Kirscke, Amy Helene. 2007. *Art in Crisis: W.E.B. Du Bois and the Struggle for African American Identity and Memory*. Bloomington, IN: Indiana University Press.

Krasner, David. 2002. *A Beautiful Pageant: African American Theatre, Drama and Performance in the Harlem Renaissance 1910–1927*. New York, NY: Palgrave McMillan.

———. 2011. *History of Modern Drama*. Hoboken, NJ: Wiley.

Lee, Josephine. 2007. "Teaching a Doll's House, Rachel and Marisol: Domestic Ideals, Possessive Individuals and Modern Drama." *Modern Drama* 50, no. 4: 620–37.

Lindsey, Treva. 2017. *Colored No More: Reinventing Black Woman in Washington D.C.* Urbana-Champaign, IL: University of Illinois Press.

Madison, D. Soyini. 1993. "That Was My Occupation: Oral Narrative, Performance and Black Feminist Thought." *Text and Performance Quarterly* 13: 213–32.

May, Vivian. 2009. "Writing the Self Into Being: Anna Julia Cooper's Textual Politics." *African American Review* 43, no. 1: 17–34.

McKibbin, Molly Littlewood. 2011. "Southern Patriarchy and the Figure of the White Woman in Gwendolyn Brooks: 'A Bronzeville Mother Loiters in Mississippi: Meanwhile, a Mississippi Mother Burns Bacon'." *African American Review* 44, no. 4: 667–85.

Miller, Ericka M. 2000. *The Other Reconstruction: Where Violence and Womanhood Meet in the Writings of Wells-Barnett, Grimke and Larsen*. New York, NY: Garland Publishing, Inc.

Mitchell, Koritha. 2011. *Living With Lynching: African American Lynching Plays, Performance and Citizenship, 1830–1930*. Urbana, IL: University of Illinois Press.

Ndounou, Monica. 2012. "Drama for Neglected People: Recovering Anna Julia Cooper's Dramatic Theory and Criticism from the Shadows of W.E.B. Du Bois and Alain Locke." *Journal of Dramatic Theory and Criticism*: 25–50.

Perkins, Kathy A., and Judith L. Stephens. 1998. *Strange Fruit: Plays on Lynching by American Women*. Bloomington, IN: Indiana University Press.

Phelan, Peggy. 1993. *Unmarked: The Politics of Performance*. London: Routledge.

Schechter, Patricia. 1997. "Unsettled Business: Ida B. Wells Against Lynching or, How Antilynching Got Its Gender." In *Under Sentence of Death: Lynching in the South*, edited by W. Fitzhugh Brundage, 293–313. Chapel Hill, NC: University of North Carolina Press.

———. 2001. *Ida B. Wells-Barnett and American Reform 1880–1930*. Chapel Hill, NC: University of North Carolina Press.

Southern, Eileen. 1983. *The Music of Black Americans: A History*. New York, NY: W.W. Norton and Company.

Stephens, Judith L. 1998. *Lynching Dramas and Women: History and Critical Conxtext*. Bloomington, IN: Indiana University Press.

———. 2006. *The Plays of Georgia Douglas Johnson: From the Negro Renaissance to the Civil Rights Movement*. Urbana-Champaign, IL: University of Illinois Press.

Terrell, Mary Church. 1904. "Lynching from a Negro's Point of View." *The North American Review* 178, no. 571: 853–68.

Turner, Victor. 1982. *From Ritual to Theatre: The Human Seriousness of Play*. New York, NY: PAJ Publications.

Wilmer, S. E. 2000. "Restaging the Nation: The Work of Suzan Lori Parks." *Modern Drama* 43, no. 3, Fall: 442–52.

Chapter 2

"Saving White Face"

Examining anti-lynching plays set in white households

Subsequent to publication of Perkins and Stephens' *Strange Fruit* anthology (1999), anti-lynching play scholarship trends toward separation by the race and gender of the playwrights, since "plays written in the anti-lynching tradition represent an important community of consciousness between black and white Americans and reveal an artistic tradition that both preserves and transcends black/white racial separation in the unity of dramatic form".[1] Both black and white playwrights used the dramatic form as a seedbed of cultural creativity[2] in order to respond to lynching performance as compulsory (state sanctioned) violence institutionalizing racialized and gendered categorizations of identity "as part of the process of consolidating Jim Crow," as a re-assertion of white supremacist patriarchy after slavery.[3] *Strange Fruit*, which provides a highly useful index of anti-lynching plays divided by the author's race and gender, facilitates close examination of anti-lynching plays as divided.[4] Examinations of anti-lynching plays written by both black and white women playwrights with the respective goals of focusing on the plays as a means of "black survival" as well as "to determine each dramatist's representation of the themes through action, stage directions or elements of characterization"[5] provide important historical context, socio-cultural analysis and character description.

While it is true that race and gender play important roles in examining anti-lynching plays, it is important to find ways to read these plays in complex ways that "preserve and transcend racial unity" rather than exacerbate racial division. Dividing anti-lynching plays by race and gender of the author is important since recovery and preservation of the modern theatre genre requires that black feminist artists receive recognition as progenitors lest lynching plays fall prey to the same racialized and gendered oppressive forces initially burying the genre. Furthermore, division along racial and gender lines is highly useful for indexing the plays; however, when critical lynching studies scholars begin to carefully consider anti-lynching plays as an early modern theatre innovation through which artists and intellectuals challenged lynching as a white supremacist performance practice, an examination of how the plays functioned as modern theatre becomes a priority. Specifically, how did the plays perform catharsis in a racist society, especially with regard to clarification and purification? Even further, when using a dramaturgical perspective to contextualize the modern Jim Crow era into which these plays were written, categorizing the plays based on race-based spatial considerations provides important subtext for the genre. Therefore, dividing the plays according to the race- based makeup of private households proves an effective way to conduct close readings of the plays, especially with regard to negotiating private performances versus public performances of whiteness, as well as examinations of how the plays perform clarification and purification.

Dividing lynching plays according to the race of the household also accounts for cross cultural depictions. Black women playwrights and adapters, including this writer, create lynching plays set in white households even though we are not white. Black women lynching dramatists such as Georgia Douglas Johnson and May Miller penned plays about white households, thereby performing as early critical lynching studies scholars who understood the role white households played within lynching performances. Additionally, Ann Seymour Link, a white woman playwright, penned *Lawd Does You Undahstan?* (1936) depicting a black household in unflattering ways. If Seymour's play were directly compared to other lynching plays set in black households, anti-lynching drama scholars can determine how black households function in the white imagination.

In this chapter, I will conduct close readings of anti-lynching plays set in white households/private spaces. I examine lynching plays in white households as sites of preliminary, embedded and subsequent lynching performances including a discussion of how these plays perform catharsis through clarification of the lynching event. Finally, anti-lynching plays are examined to reveal the ways white women's performances figure into them to contrast with the ways they are represented in "the lynching story."

Lynching plays set in white households

Lynching plays set in white households foreground these environs as principal settings within the lynching cycle, including three classes: preliminary, embedded or subsequent performances. According to performance studies scholar Kirk Fuoss:

> Preliminary performances occur between the alleged precipitating crime and the mob's seizure of its victim. Embedded performances occur after the mob's seizure of its victim and include all performances up to and including extralegal public execution. Finally, subsequent performances include all those that happen after the event.[6]

Lynching dramas set in white homes can be examined as realms in which the lynching cycle, especially preliminary and subsequent performances, is depicted through unethical, abusive behavior such as domestic violence between white men and white women, psychological abuse of black employees, as well as duping and scapegoating innocent black men. Performances of white women are also foregrounded, whether they are depicted as critical thinkers, as objectified and unaware or as principal bearers of the white supremacist tradition. Lynching plays in white households unmask these whiteness performance realms as private domains in which public lynching performances are deeply rooted, effectively (re)producing lynching ideology.

Tracy Mygatt's The Noose

Tracy Mygatt's *The Noose*, the earliest written lynching play set in a white household, dramatizes a privileged white woman's efforts to combat lynching performances. First produced between April and May 1919 in Manhattan at the Neighborhood Playhouse on Grand Street,[7] *The Noose* followed up Grimke's *Rachel*, marking anti-lynching plays as a site of coalitional politics between black and white women.[8] By echoing Grimke's play, Mygatt demonstrated an early willingness to accept white women's complicity in lynching performances prefiguring the anti-lynching efforts of Jessie Daniel Ames, who in 1930, founded the Association of Southern Women for the Prevention of Lynching (ASWPL), an activist group for white women.[9] In her article, "Whiteness and Political Purpose in *The Noose*, an Anti-Lynching Play by Tracy Mygatt," Frances Early provides a detailed overview of the play, observing: "Mygatt sought to disrupt and critique the largely unexamined ideological assumptions embedded in notions of whiteness and civilization, gender, and class that hindered political efforts for racial justice in early twentieth-century US society."[10] Early directly ties *The Noose* to Mygatt's other writing as well as her pre-World War I pro-democratic and peace activism. In this section, I will conduct a reading of the play using Early's description, focusing on identifying lynching's performance cycle as depicted within the drama as well as the communicative strategies Mygatt uses to challenge lynching as discursive and material whiteness performance practice. Finally, I will discuss Mygatt's depiction of white women's anti-lynching performance practices.

Tracy (Dickinson) Mygatt (1885–1973) is best known as an "ardent pacifist" for her lifelong anti-war activism, including her protest of World War I and cofounding the War Resisters League (WRL) with Frances Witherspoon in 1923. Mygatt graduated from Bryn Mawr College in 1908 and became a member of the Socialist party in 1913 upon her and Witherspoon's move to New York where they became active in many socialist, suffrage and pacifist organizations. Mygatt and Witherspoon lived and worked so closely until their deaths in 1973 that the non-normative pairing is rarely cited without each other. In 1917, Witherspoon founded, with Mygatt's help, the Bureau of Legal Advice[11] which advocated for civil liberties during the World War I era. During this time, Mygatt "authored or coauthored a number of books, many of them with anti-war themes"[12] as well as two dramas whose theme developed as outgrowths of her political activism. In addition to *Good Friday* (1919), a play "based on a true story of the torture and death in Alcatraz military prison of a religious conscientious objector,"[13] Mygatt wrote *The Noose*, reflecting her insight into a tie between lynching and war as whiteness performance practice. *The Noose* can also be viewed as a development based on her relationships with Witherspoon through which she gained first-hand exposure to Southern whiteness performances. Mygatt's association with Mary Ovington, a founder of the NAACP, and Martha Gruening, a lawyer and journalist who served as a key member of the NAACP's staff early in its establishment, are also found to be influential to her writing. Much like Ovington's short story "The White Brute,"[14] *The Noose* counteracts lynching as whiteness performance by inverting the image of "the black brute" to depict and discuss (common) instances of white men's rape of black women for which no one was punished.

According to Frances Early's close description, *The Noose* is set in a fictional Southern town, Warino, Georgia, on Christmas Eve at the home of Mr. and Mrs. Henry Clay, a privileged, Southern white couple. Mr. Clay is a prominent, well-connected attorney while Mrs. Clay is portrayed as a middle aged, severely racist homemaker. In the play's opening scene, Mrs. Clay displays a patronizing cruelty toward her black servant, Peter Johnson, especially after he requests to stay the night in the attic of the Clay home to avoid an impending lynching. Mrs. Clay refuses his request as that of a "cowardly nigger" who, like all others, needs to be "taught" through lynching. Mrs. Clay's berating subjects him to a torture tactic of psychological abuse, in which she anchors his need for a safe place to stay overnight to white power, invoked through her allusion to lynching performance as a pedagogical strategy. Elaine Scarry explains,

> Torture is a parallel act of deconstruction. It imitates the destructive power of war: rather than destroying the concrete physical fact of streets, houses, factories and schools, it destroys them as they exist in the mind of the prisoner, it destroys them as they exist in the furnishings of a room: to convert a table into a weapon is to set a factory on fire; to hear a confession is to watch from above the explosion of a city block.[15]

Furthermore, through Mrs. Clay's actions the audience is immediately made aware of the Clay household as a chamber in which black people are targeted as "internal" enemies who are subjected to torture in contrast to war which "more often arises where the enemy is external, occupies a separate space, where the impulse to obliterate a rival population and its civilization is not (or need not be perceived as) a self-destruction."[16] The (white) Clay household in *The Noose* is depicted as a house of "drama" or where destruction of blacks is "acted out symbolically within a handful of rooms." Mrs. Clay's opening speech acts function as a preliminary lynching performance since her performance foreshadows her son's soon to follow actions.

Mrs. Clay continues her psychological torture tactics by demanding that Peter retrieve the family's Bible "in preparation for prayers when her husband, 'the master,' returns."[17] By referring to her husband as "master," Mrs. Clay infers a pre-Civil War/Emancipation master-slave relationship between her husband and Peter. Although slavery is over, Mrs. Clay continues to perform as if the practice still exists. Even further, she layers her verbal art with race-based insults, false claims of pedagogical charity, as well as a performance of Christian, moral superiority. As such, Mygatt depicts Mrs. Clay's white supremacist performance as largely made up of unethical discursive strategies through which she commits acts of domestic violence toward the blacks who work for her. The Clay household is also depicted as an unregulated work environment in which black workers are subjected to (at least) verbal and psychological abuse. Although they are continually being provoked, black domestic workers are keenly aware of the violence threatening them and, in order to avoiding the violence, assume a physical posture of deference. Although Mrs. Clay refers to Peter's manner as "weak," his survival strategy of allowing the verbal abuse to go unchallenged keeps him alive. The audience is also witness to the process by which psychological torture "destroys a person's world, self and voice."[18]

In contrast, when Margaret, Mrs. Clay's daughter-in-law arrives, Mrs. Clay is easily disarmed by a fellow white woman who does not subscribe to her same performance values. The women's differing communicative values are revealed through an exchange they engage in soon after Margaret's entrance and initial greetings, which includes a handshake with Peter. When Margaret asks about the whereabouts of her husband, Houston (Hugh), Mrs. Clay tries to distract her by trying to impress her with news that a high-ranking state politician from Atlanta has recently sent Hugh a letter. Margaret, who is not easily distracted, critically responds to the unsolicited information:

> Why, isn't he the state boss? . . . Well, I don't see what that kind of person has to say to Hugh. . . . McCormick soils everything he touches! I know how interested Hugh is in politics – I've felt it in him all these years we've been married, though I reckon – [with a little laugh] I reckon I know better than to talk to him about it! – but it's clean politics he cares about – not pitch.[19]

Margaret's expression of disdain for McCormick's "pitch"-based politics in favor of "clean politics" depicts a difference in political values between the two women. Margaret distinguishes McCormick's political performance as "pitch," indicating a focus on surface or superficiality quality by which she is not impressed, no matter McCormick's title and/or rank. In fact, Margaret ascribes to McCormick a dirty or defiled status which is a marked contrast, ironic even, considering Mrs. Clay had recently presented herself as a woman of high moral stature who presumably wouldn't be associated with or impressed by a dirty politician such as McCormick. We can also note here that Margaret's willingness to shake hands with Peter diverges from Mrs.

Clay's treatment of him with the intent of marking him with negative characteristics or conferring upon him contaminated status. In this moment, Margaret identifies herself as an antiracist white woman who chooses her company by one's content of character rather than the color of their skin, an idea that foreshadows Martin Luther King Jr.'s epic phrasing by more than 50 years.

Margaret and Mrs. Clay's conversation, which Early describes as "didactic,"[20] proceeds to include Margaret's explanation of why her mother refuses to visit her own hometown any more, even discouraging Margaret from marrying men from the town or the South in general. As a girl of 16, Margaret's mother witnessed the lynching of an innocent man – a lynching Margaret's grandfather, the local sheriff, is unable to thwart. Margaret's mother is forever after affected by the actions of the town's most respected white citizens who participated in a race riot, terrorizing young black men for several days afterward. Margaret's retelling of the historical lynching event foreshadows the present events of which she is still unaware. Soon thereafter, a lynch mob's flaming red glow passes her "French windows" and she realizes that a lynching is presently happening. She tries to run outside to intervene but is stopped by Peter who informs her that it is too late since the victim is already dead.

Houston Clay returns home and Margaret is initially relieved to see him, thinking she will find comfort from her outrage in him. Soon, however, she puts two and two together and realizes that Hugh has participated as a member of the lynch mob with their daughter in tow, even justifying his behavior, as Early details:

> Some day Jeannie will be a woman, Houston continues, and 'with all these new-fangled Yankee ideas goin' about, we can't train her too early to . . . be a true daughter of the South!' Like 'every one of the best people' in Warino, Houston claims to have performed his 'duty' when he and others 'strung up a nigger' in defense of white women's honor.[21]

Houston and Margaret then enter into a heated ideological discussion which, according to Early, "represents the thematic center of the play." Through Margaret's argument with Hugh, Mygatt uses a Socratic method of questioning to probe Hugh's assumptions about "the black brute" image he unthinkingly invokes. Margaret attempts to make explicit Hugh's biases, assumptions and logical fallacies used as justifications for lynching. When Hugh invokes an (stereotypical) image of "the black brute" as reproduced through a traditional white supremacist narrative, "the lynching story," Margaret shoots back at him, "And who taught them first? Who stole their wives and daughters, and after they had used them, sold them on the block like cattle? Answer me that, Houston! Answer me that!"[22] Here, Margaret questions a white supremacist cultural logic that black brutes emerge out of thin blue air; a reasoning that assumes that "black brutes" are not imitating "white brutes" who kidnapped and raped black women with a regularity evidenced, according to Margaret, by disproportionate number of mulattoes born to black women versus those born to white women. Mygatt probes even deeper into assumptions ungirding "the black brute" to question an applied exploitative practice of selling brutalized black women and children as slave labor, raising a complex yet little discussed fact about slavery: it's operation as a structure "of captivity and abjection through gendered capitalism." In unearthing "the development of systems of terror, structures of economic and political subordination and hidden dimensions of working class African American women's lives," Sarah Haley traces to slavery a reworked and extended system of "gendered racial capitalism"[23] making a New South possible. According to Haley, Jim Crow modernity was predicated on emergent modes of "gender and sexual ideology" which were institutionalized through the imprisonment of black women who were subjected to unregulated violence and exploited labor practices. Interestingly, Haley's study heavily references a state prison in Milledgeville, Georgia, the state in which *The Noose* is also set.

Margaret and Hugh go on to debate a propensity for rape among all males as well as white people's role in civilizing black people. However, both arguments reflect another side, a nefarious proposition that Southern white men and women are themselves uncivilized and it is their own lack of humanity that is projected onto black bodies through discursive and material rape and lynching. Even further, the guilt or innocence of "the black brute" is further brought into question when two of Hugh's associates arrive and it is strongly suggested that Warren Fite, the owner of the mill where the raped girl worked, actually committed the crime. An allusion to the innocence of the black lynching victim echoes Margaret's earlier recounting of the innocence of the black lynching victim killed when her mother lived in the town. Fite's inappropriate, drunken behavior embarrasses Hugh who tries to remove Fite from the house; however, Margaret doesn't let Hugh disassociate himself from his co-murderer so easily.

Eventually, over Hugh's protestations, it is Margaret who leaves the house as well as her marriage to Hugh, retrieving her daughter from the Henderson's and returning to her mother's Virginia home. In protest to Hugh's role in the lynching, Margaret commits a non-traditional act of leaving her husband even though we soon learn that Hugh will be rewarded with the state governorship for his participation. As earlier referenced by Margaret in the conversation with Mrs. Clay, she is unwilling to be a part of "dirty," lynching-based politics.

Mygatt's depiction of a direct link between lynching and political elections, especially with regard to the practice's function as a bonding ritual between white men that in effect functioned as a pre-qualifying ritual for elected office, exemplifies the ways anti-lynching plays set in white households effectively provided "intellectual clarification" for lynching performances as modern drama *par excellence*. Mygatt's clarification of lynching performances as qualifying practices for elevation to "elected" offices in Southern states reveals the practice as functioning in the same ways as lynching photographs and souvenirs. Lynching performances are now understood as a white supremacist performance ritual used as an affective bonding ritual among powerful, white, male, "dirty" politicians. When McCormick presents Hugh Clay with the noose used in the commission of the lynching, presumably functioning as a trophy or souvenir, Clay is forever marked as "dirty." Contrary to Hugh's mother's performance ideology associating black people with defilement, it is her son Hugh that is marked by such a grotesque designation, not the black people who work for her.

Although *The Noose* cannot be directly traced to the writing of black women that proceeds the play by some 20 years, Mygatt's intellectual and political background make it easy to tie her writing to black women's anti-lynching theory. Tracy Mygatt's clarification of lynching performances as a cover up for raping black women and girls mirrors the (public) intellectual cultural production of Ida B. Wells-Barnett and Mary Church Terrell. Margaret's refusal to allow herself or her daughter association with Southern white racist performances reiterates refusal as a black feminist strategy used by Grimke's protagonist in *Rachel*. In these ways, Mygatt shows a willingness to cooperate with the efforts of black people in fighting against race, gender, social and economic oppression. Mygatt's interracial coalitional politics evidences anti-lynching plays as non-traditional, integrated theatre in which black and white households performed as split subjects, mirroring each other in order to clarify lynching performances as functioning to mask the rape of black women and girls as well as the abuse and exploitation of black labor.

Corrie Crandall Howell's *The Forfeit*

Corrie Crandall Howell's *The Forfeit* also depicts a preliminary lynching performance taking place in a white domestic setting; this time, the result is a duping and scapegoating of an innocent black male, Jeff, who works as a farmhand for Tom Clark, a white man. According to Perkins and Stephens, the date of the play and all information about its author could not be located indicating possible use of a pseudonym.[24] The drama centers upon Clark's wife, Fanny, who seeks to cover up a local rape and murder committed by her reckless son, Bud. As bloodhounds and a lynch mob approach her house, she quickly executes a plan that frames Jeff into taking the fall for the crime. Jeff, who is unaware of the crime, comes by to deliver potatoes and is lured into the Clark home. When Jeff questions her upon hearing the barking bloodhounds, Fanny feigns ignorance, telling him hunters must be, "Rabbit huntin, I reckon."[25] When the mob, led by Fanny's husband, Tom, finally arrives, Fanny hides Bud and turns Jeff over as the guilty party. Fanny knows that, by virtue of the crime committed and Jeff's skin color, Jeff is presumed guilty. Since the victim is dead, there is no eye witness to dispute Fanny's lies.

In *The Forfeit*, duping and scapegoating constitute preliminary lynching performances taking place in white households when evidence leads to white assailants. Knowing full well of her son's guilt, Fanny first dupes Jeff into staying present until the mob arrives. Then, in order to cover up for her son, she scapegoats Jeff as the murderer. Fanny performs as a "false witness" to a crime, a criminal offense for which she, as a white woman, will not be held accountable. Interestingly, Fanny's preliminary lynching performances are closely related to those that "stage(d) rapes" or when white women posed as rape victims for attention or to cover up their own illicit liaisons. Often, innocent black people were lynched before this "staging" could be discovered.[26] We can also rightly conclude that many innocents, like Jeff, were lynched without these preliminary performances ever being discovered since lynched victims are completely denied judicial due process where such inconsistencies might be detected.

Furthermore, Fanny, a middle-aged white woman, is depicted as lead performer or active bearer in the lynching performance tradition, since it is Fanny who knowingly misleads law enforcement officials. In this way, Crandall depicts white women as anything but passive victims in need of rescuing per "the lynching story." On the contrary, white women purposely activate and expedite lynching performances, especially with regard to committing misdirection and lying to cover up for white guilty parties. Fanny's performance reveals white women's non-normative performance in lynching. Contrary to "the lynching story," Fanny is revealed to be anything but mentally and physically helpless when it comes to protecting herself and her household. In fact, not only is she depicted as interacting with a black man in a non-sexual way in which she doesn't feel threatened, Fanny knows of and abuses her narrative power over Jeff to commit domestic violence against him as a preliminary lynching performance. As we saw in *The Noose*, a black male laborer who works in a white domestic setting is depicted as subject to domestic abuse; in *The Forfeit*, however, Fanny's "range of speech activity"[27] goes beyond verbal abuse to include implicating Jeff in a crime he did not commit resulting in his death by lynching.

May Miller's *Nails and Thorns*

Per Perkins and Stephens, as well as Lindsey, May Miller (1899–1995) is identified as the key figure in the study of lynching plays. As the daughter of a Howard University dean and sociology professor, Miller's birth and upbringing in an educational setting effectively set her up for success as a Progressive Era playwright, poet and teacher. Miller wrote her first play, *Pandora's Box*, at the tender age of 15 as an M Street High School student while studying under both Angelina Weld Grimke and Mary Burrill. Miller attended college at Howard University where she flourished amidst the establishment by Alain Locke and Montgomery T. Gregory of The Howard Players, the first drama program for black students.[28] Upon her 1920 graduation she was awarded an inaugural playwriting award for *Within the Shadows*, a one-act drama. Miller went on to teach at Baltimore's Frederick Douglas High School while she also performed and directed as a member of Krigwa Players, a Negro Little Theatre group started by W.E.B. Du Bois. Informally, Miller's professional development was enriched by her fellowship as a regular attendee at Georgia Douglas Johnson's S Street Salon. According to diary entries which are housed among a collection of her correspondence, poetry and dramatic writing, scrapbooks of student work and personal legal papers at Emory University's Stuart A. Rose Manuscript, Archives and Rare Book

Library Miller, Johnson and Willis Richardson shared a closeness and consistency since to them she often referred.[29] In fact, Miller and Richardson eventually co-edited an anthology of "Negro History" plays for which Carter G. Woodson wrote an introduction.[30] Miller regularly submitted her plays to black publications; she also shared correspondence with Dillard University's S. Edmonds Randolph who, in 1936, expressed dissatisfaction with her third place award from the Association for Southern Women for the Prevention of Lynching (ASWPL)'s playwriting contest. Although there is no official record of production for *Nails and Thorns*,[31] Randolph expressed his support of her work by reporting his staging of her play *Harry Tubman* (sic) for which he'd previously submitted a requisition for a five dollar royalty payment as well as vowing to stage *Nails and Thorns* sometime during the same year.[32]

Nails and Thorns, a one-act lynching play, effectively represents how black and white women's respective performances mirror each other in a whiteness lynching culture that, despite a melodramatic rhetoric of heroism, leaves no subject unharmed. Gladys Landers, a local sheriff's wife, is a nervous wreck due to a Negro's alleged assault on a white woman that has just taken place in her hometown, "a small town – probably South-probably West – small town ruled by frenzy."[33] Gladys begs her husband to notify the governor of the impending lynching, but he downplays her fears. When Annabel, their African American servant, arrives, Annabel echoes Gladys' instincts, especially since Annabel has first-hand testimony of the reign of terror now being demonstrated upon the town's black residents. Even further, Annabel details compelling evidence proving that the lynching will definitely take place and that there exists a specific plan for carrying it out. What had only been the threat of a lynching is now a reality. At first, Gladys tries to deny Annabel's perspective, but she finally admits that Annabel's insights are a confirmation of her own. When Gladys tells Annabel of her plans to take her baby son with her to thwart the mob's activities, Annabel parallels their experiences: "I'd hide may sons an' you'd bed hide your'n till those folks git some sense."[34] Gladys goes against Annabel's warning resulting in the mob trampling the white child to death.

Miller's depiction of the reckless murder of Gladys' child by a white lynch mob characterizes the mob's carnival atmosphere as a modern "ritual spectacle" which according to Mikhail Bakhtin, "resist, exaggerate and destabilize the distinctions and boundaries that mark and maintain high culture and organized society."[35] During lynching performances, the mob acts as if all semblance of American high culture, including the United States Constitution, democracy, justice as well as human ethics, moral and legal codes are "ingested . . . and released . . . in fits and starts in all manner of recombination, inversion, mockery, and degradation."[36] Bakhtin critiques modern carnival "as a radical diminishment of the possibilities of human freedom and cultural production." Within the context of American lynching culture, Miller foregrounds white motherhood as an abject subject position, destabilizing it as a cultural ideal, facilitating empathy for black mothers for whom such horror is an imminent grotesque reality. Miller also models affectivity between white mothers and black mothers through a relationship between Gladys and Annabel who is Gladys' only source of comfort after her infant is killed.[37]

Contrary to modern representations rendering her an unreliable witness due to her race, gender and class, in Miller's *Nails and Thorns*, Annabel is recognized as dependable and trustworthy. White women are characterized, through Gladys, not as shy and quiet, but as staunch, anti-lynching advocates, critical thinkers who expose the ways lynching harms "every soul in town," not only actual lynching victim(s). When performing lynching, Gladys observes, (white) townspeople crucified "everything that was worthwhile – justice and pride and self-respect. For generations to come the children will be gathering the nails and thorns from the scene of that crucifixion."[38] Annabel and Gladys, directly and indirectly, support each other as fellow mothers who are concerned with the future of their children. Not only do their onstage images mirror each other, an offstage dynamic between black and white women anti-lynching activists is mirrored here, as well. I would also argue that the murder of Gladys' infant occurs in the same manner as Mary Turner's unborn child, although Gladys' life is spared.[39] For her creative effort, May Miller was awarded a prize by the Association for Southern Women for the Prevention of Lynching (ASWPL),[40] who, under the leadership of Jessie Daniel Ames, targeted white audiences in their efforts to eradicate lynching since she believed it wasn't possible for whites to be persuaded by blacks. Ames' organization mirrored the campaigns launched by black women's clubs as well as the NAACP.

Miller's non-normative portrayal of white women's subjectivity in lynching culture functions to disrupt the lynching performance cycle within white households. Interestingly, *Nails and Thorns* foregrounds a thinking white woman subject in a similar manner as Tracy Mygatt's main character, Margaret. Both playwrights use white households as settings in which to illustrate white women as concerned citizens who understand lynching as an event by which everyone in the community is affected, not just black people. Also, both characters challenge a politics of white respectability in seeking to thwart a perpetuation of white supremacy; Margaret does so by leaving her husband while Gladys tries to individually confront a mob in lieu of her husband's neglect of his duties as sheriff. Finally, both lynching plays show active white women of childbearing age interacting with black women and men domestics in humane, non-exploitative ways, even showing respect for black people's thoughts and opinions. Miller's work also reflects a concern with reproductive rights among both black and white women. Even further, I am interested in how May Miller's other literary depictions of white women and households cross reference this counter hegemonic strategy, especially with regard to whiteness as property. Further study of Miller's work across genres is called for, in order to compare and contrast the many ways she subverts "the lynching story" through her literary representation of white female subjects.

Judge Lynch by J. W. Rogers

Judge Lynch (1923), written by John William (J.W.) Rogers (1894–1965) was first performed by the Green Mask Players in Houston, Texas. Next, on May 1, 1924, the Dallas Little Theatre Players performed the one-act play at New York City's Belasco Theatre where it won the first Little Theater competition's "Belasco Cup," making Rogers an "overnight success." Born in Dallas, Texas, Rogers developed an interest in drama while a student at Dartmouth. After college, Rogers worked in the advertising and publishing fields in New York before completing an 18-month term of service in the military during World War I. Rogers returned to Dallas after the war where he worked as a newspaperman. His other plays include *Dark Blood* which was distinguished as being the first play produced with no characters on stage. Rogers was also well known for his interviews with famous writers, including F. Scott Fitzgerald as well as for his book, *The Lusty Texans of Dallas*. *Judge Lynch* was included in Locke and Montgomery's anthology, *Plays of Negro Life* (1927).[41]

Judge Lynch opens with a lynching already in progress. Ed Joplin is away from his home as part of a lynch mob in pursuit of "the Jacks nigger," for allegedly murdering Squire Tatum. His mother, Mrs. Joplin, is comforting Ed's wife, Ella, about his absence. She does so by reassuring Ella of their safety while Ed is away; they have her absent husband's gun. Mrs. Joplin also declares Ed's participation in the lynching to be part of his "duty," invoking an image of an unredeemable "nigger" who needs to be trained "to live in a Christian land" as a means of affective bonding with her daughter-in-law. Mrs. Joplin confidently prophesies, "They'll get that nigger, though. They always do. It'll be a terrible death he'll die, but he brought it on himself. It does look like niggers would learn, but I reckon they wouldn't be niggers if they did." Ella remembers that she can't blame Ed for leaving her and Mrs. Joplin at the house since the last lynching in the county happened ten years prior and he'd missed it. The women comfort each other in Ed's absence by telling each other different versions of "the lynching story."

Contradictions abound with regard to this particular lynching as an exercise of justice. As opposed to a "black brute," the victim is known to be hard-working, kind and polite, timid even. Squire Tatum is well known to have a bad temper set off by the least little thing anybody, whether black or white, does. Although the women note such inconsistencies, they are shockingly uncritical of the story being used to justify lynching reflecting how "the lynching story" escapes any scrutiny in everyday conversation. Even though their intimate knowledge of those involved doesn't square up with (a version of) "the lynching story" used to justify the current manhunt (and all the others), the women disregard their own understanding and, unquestioningly, transition into their chores. In doing so, Ella and Mrs. Joplin show how "the lynching story" is affectively reproduced into their daily lives.

"A Stranger" soon appears, startling Ella. He turns out to be a "snake-oil" salesman, seeking to sell the woman a secret "Indian" potion that will help them perform their chores better. The Stranger's sales pitch reflects an emerging tradition in American advertising of using people of color's "exoticism" to sell products to ignorant consumers. Interestingly, the Stranger's sales pitch is juxtaposed to "the lynching story" as an emerging whiteness narrative technique in which the image of people of color is exploited and slandered in order to sell a product or idea. After flattering the women, the Stranger is just transitioning into his call to action when Ed returns homes and completely distracts the women with an eyewitness account of the lynching.

Upon his return, Ed begins a (competing) tale about details of the lynching performance or, as Ed refers to it, the "ketch." As opposed to a black woman's retelling of events, a white man "narrativizes the lynching," as subsequent lynching performance. In the same way that the phrase, "once upon a time" signals to an audience the beginning of an Indo-European fairy tale, Ed's verbal art is "keyed" by his seemingly calm demeanor (which Rogers indicates as "still struggling to appear unmoved") and hand washing. Rogers also indicates Ed's narrative performance through strict choreography of interaction between Mrs. Joplin and Ed as well as a reference to the speech act as a "recital." Mrs. Joplin and Ed obviously enter into a well-rehearsed dynamic as he washes blood from his hands and she appears to hand him a towel, as if on cue, although every effort is made to appear as improvised. Even further, Ed goes on to detail a complex of several "coincidences" that made carrying out the lynching easy: "That warn't hard," Ed observes when Ella asked how "the ketch" was made. Ed recounts a sequence of occurrences such as a mob arriving at a particular location (Squire's place) at the exact same time, as well as a concise, formulaic narrative indicting and convicting "the nigger" of the murder in one fell swoop.

Ed's "narrativization" begins to shift as he describes the final part of the lynching's preliminary performance in which the growing mob forces "the nigger's" wife to tell them where her husband is by threatening to whip her with "a big blacksnake whip" not to leave "an inch of skin on her brown body." With skepticism, Ed reports that the victim's wife said she knew nothing about the murder although she does provide the information they seek regarding her husband's whereabouts. Although the black woman's recounting is complete and detailed, the lynch mob, which now numbers 50, immediately disregards her alibi and a manhunt ensues.

The mob finds their victim, "the nigger," squirrel hunting, just as they'd been told by his wife, highlighting her credibility. However, "the show must go on" for the lynch mob, since they will not be delayed or deterred from a lynching for one moment in order to appreciate the integrity of the black woman's words. As part of an embedded lynching performance, the lynch mob performs a mock trial in which they appropriate certain aspects of an actual trial while denying the victim a fair trial. Taken another way, the lynch mob could be said to "mock" justice or makes a mockery of justice by beating the victim while coercing a confession from him by presenting him with two options: confessing and being killed by hanging or not confessing and killing him by burning. Through Ed's delivery of an extended monologue, every part of the mock trial is made explicit. Ed's embedded performance is an aberration from many accounts of lynching which "indicate that mock trials occurred" but "provide few details." In *Judge Lynch*, the audience, including the Stranger, is made privy to the mock trial as a scene in the play which elucidates lynching as a complex of discursive performances which culminates in an excessive mutilation of the body; in this case, the victim's body is hanged from a tree and riddled with bullets, "full er bullets as a rake is full er teeth." Through their oratorical performances justifying lynching, lynchers claimed to stand "for law and order and justice," while also deeming themselves as "God fearing, law abiding citizens" all while committing acts of debasement such as referring to the victim as a "low down black scoundrel" and "a black baboon." Such contradictions make clear that these embedded performances "functioned as pre-emptive arguments that attempted to undermine the an-innocent-person-was lynched claim before anti-lynching activists even had a chance to advance the claim."[42]

Upon hearing of the victim's "confession" and the actual details of Squire's murder, the Stranger becomes visibly upset and horrified. Although the audience is now aware that something is wrong with the Stranger, Ella resumes the subsequent performance of Ed's retelling of events. Ella asks questions about a funeral as well as a follow-up about recovery of the dead white man's stolen watch. Ed responds in the negative, since the mob thoroughly searched the victim's person for the watch yet did not find it. Of course, Ella blames the victim, suggesting that he and his wife together conspired to conceal the watch. As indicated in the script, the Stranger is visibly frustrated and angry due to his inability to exit without notice as well as his memory of Squire whose "powerful mean temper" Ella and Ed recall, even admitting his "nasty way with strangers." Just when the Stranger finds a moment to make his escape, Mrs. Joplin stops him to let him know that she's noticed his incredible discomfort. Instead of following up on her observations, however, Mrs. Joplin makes excuses for the Stranger's reaction while also taking the time to justify her son's participation in the lynching mob. Mrs. Joplin performs her (more comprehensive) version of "the lynching story" which includes a dehumanization of blacks due to their African origins and the fear of whites with which whites must now, in a post slavery era, contend. She also includes a reference to caged animals in the circus to whom she compares blacks in their reaction to their captivity. Even as the Stranger struggles mightily to maintain his composure regarding the dead white man's horrible temper while mentioning the possibility that he was murdered justifiably as indicated by all who knew him (including his wife), Mrs. Joplin is still unable to comprehend the meaning of the Stranger's words, blinded by an incongruity with the whiteness narratives she regularly performs. What's worse is that when Ella finds Squire's missing watch on a wood pile that the audience has seen the Stranger mistakenly drop in his rush to get away, both she and her mother-in-law can only conclude that "the nigger" must've come close to their house and dropped it versus correctly deducing that the only visitor to their farmhouse that day, the white stranger/salesperson, is the real killer.

Like other lynching plays set in white households, *Judge Lynch* provides catharsis through clarification of the lynching event. Although the white family of lynchers appears unaware of their whiteness performances, Rogers makes it clear to the audience that Mrs. Joplin, Ella and Ed act uncritically in their commission and justification of the murder of an innocent black man. The injustice is compounded by a visit to their home by the actual murderer whom they entertain with a subsequent lynching performance instead of holding him accountable for the murder of their neighbor. By clarifying a lynching event in this way, *Judge Lynch* performs catharsis for an audience who actually subscribes to American ideals of justice but is unsure about why the ideal cannot be realized.

A Sunday morning in the South (white church version and black church version) by Georgia Douglas Johnson

Georgia Douglas Johnson, the genre's most prolific contributor, is the only lynching playwright to outright produce two race-based iterations of the same play, *A Sunday Morning in the South*. One version of the lynching play, a white church version, is made up of two acts while the other is a one-act play set in a black church. Both plays revolve around a cast of black characters, a non-traditional family made up of an elderly grandmother, Sue Jones, and her two grandsons, Tom and Bossie, aged 19 and 7 respectively. Sue's friend Liza visits the household in both versions of the play as well as two officers and a white girl. However, the white church version includes an usher and a judge, Robert Manning, who do not appear in the black church version. The black church version includes a second family friend, a black woman named Matilda who is a little younger than the other two women.

Both the white and black church versions open in Sue Jones' kitchen where she's just finished preparing breakfast for her grandsons whom she beckons to the table. In the white church version Sue wears a blue bandana handkerchief to cover her hair and a brown gingham apron tied at her waist while in the black church version she wears a red bandana and blue gingham apron. Sue moves with a limp to indicate rheumatism in the white version; in the black version she actually uses a cane. She soon begins to chastise Tom for his slowness to which he retorts that he's still recovering from the previous working day which was long and backbreaking. Sympathizing with him, she regrets not rubbing "snake oil liniment" on his back before he went to bed but remembers that she was unable to since he fell asleep before she finished the supper dishes when she could come to his aid. Tom affirms that his exhaustion put him to sleep well before 8 o'clock. Just as Bossie sits down and begins to "one up" his brother with talk of his future as a preacher who will escape such back breaking work, Liza comes over to share coffee and a biscuit as well as news of a manhunt for a black man accused of rape. Sue and Bossie enter into a clarifying discussion about rape allegations in which white women accuse black men, passing off the accusation as a lie. Liza even cites a lynching occurring in Texas the previous year in which it was afterward discovered that the alleged crime was actually committed by a white man who first "blacked his face." Johnson here refers to burnt cork crimes, a preliminary lynching performance through which white criminals scapegoat innocent blacks. Sue and Liza express their wish to overcome their illiteracy in order to advocate against such injustice. Upon echoing his intention to become educated so he can help his people, black people, escape lynching, Tom wonders aloud if he would ever be a lynching victim. His grandmother assures him that it could never happen to him due to his harmlessness. Before Tom can rebut his grandmother's reasoning, a police officer knocks on the door and enters before he can be greeted. The officer immediately asks Tom about his identity, naming him and asking about his whereabouts at 10 o'clock the night before. Sue quickly provides Tom's alibi, backed up by his little brother, Bossie. The police officer offhandedly dismisses Sue's word telling her to shut up and accuses her and Bossie of lying on Tom's behalf. After reading a description of the alleged perpetrator aloud, a second officer leads in a white girl who hesitatingly identifies Tom as her attacker: "He looks something like him." The first officer unethically leads the witness by observing that Tom matches the attacker's description perfectly, implicating black neighbors who he says told him that Tom's route home from work directly passes the scene of the crime. Coerced to answer, the white girl stutters an affirmative response, covering her face as the second police officer leads her out. Tom is immediately handcuffed. Sue tries to intervene in the arrest, observing that the white girl has made a mistake since she probably thinks all blacks look alike anyway. Trying to be brave, Tom assures his grandmother that he will return soon after he explains to the sheriff about his whereabouts. The police officer condescendingly assures her that her grandson has nothing to worry about if he's innocent, referring to her as "old woman" and "Grannie." Tom is led out while Sue collapses in a chair, sobbing. Bossie falls to his grandmother's feet wondering what will happen to his brother.

The first scene of the white church version ends as Liza finds out and reports to Sue of a gathering mob's plans to lynch Tom. They brainstorm for an intervention, deciding to appeal to a "good white man" to intervene on Tom's behalf. They decide to find Judge Robert Manning no matter where they have to look.

Scene Two takes place outside a white church were Sunday service is in process. Sue and Liza run up to the church doorsteps to plead with the usher to summon Judge Manning for a life and death matter. The usher repeatedly discourages them from interrupting the judge's church worship but is finally convinced when Sue tells him she will go get him herself. Sue is anxious; she knows time is of the essence so when the judge comes to the door she hurriedly explains the circumstances to him, trying to convince him all at once of her dependence on his help as well as her grandson's innocence. Like the white police officer and usher before him, the judge minimizes Sue's request, further delaying the only hope for a lynching intervention that Sue so desperately seeks. After a volley of requests, the judge relents to going with Sue as soon as he returns from retrieving his hat. Sue tries to flatter him in order to persuade him not to waste more time and although her charm works to a certain extent, he goes to get the hat anyways. In the minute or two the judge is gone, two white men pass by, bragging about lynching Tom. When the judge returns with his hat, he finds a distraught Bossie kneeling over his grandmother's dead body; Sue is dead from a massive heart attack.

In Johnson's black church version, the family gathering at the breakfast table is queued by ringing church bells indicating the beginning of the black church's worship services. Tom expresses regret that he cannot attend due to his strained back, an injury he incurred while lifting heavy boxes by himself since Mr. John, his white boss, was nowhere to be found when Tom figured out how heavy the boxes really were. By the time Tom gets home, he is in pain and exhausted. So much so, in fact, that he miscalculates the time it took him to fall asleep by a whole hour! Sue corrects him about his bedtime (8 o'clock versus 9 o'clock) while Bossie teases Tom about his loud snoring. When Bossie asks for more breakfast he tells his grandmother that the first helping is "gone down the red lane struttin'" as he rubs his belly. Grandma Sue pretends to ignore Bossie's *Signifyin'*,[43] reminding him that until he starts working, his food portions are restricted.

Liza stops by on her way to church; in this black version she and Sue dialogue more extensively about the condition of Sue's leg. We find out that Sue will never walk on it again and that church members shun her due to its deteriorating condition. The women stop talking to listen to the choir sing "Amazing Grace" which is easily heard due to the church's close proximity. They soon resume their conversation as Liza delivers her report about the manhunt. In contrast to their after-breakfast conversation in the white church version, Sue and Liza discuss their abiding belief in law and order, including due process, as a way of ensuring innocent people aren't wrongly punished. Not only do they cite examples in which "burnt cork crimes" are committed, the women counteract "the lynching story's" claim that lynchings occur due to rapes of white women by black men, citing the lynching of Zeb Brooks as an instance in which a lynching occurred due to a dispute between a black worker and his white boss. Tom chimes in, again wondering if he could ever succumb to lynching. Liza and Sue both assure him of his status in the community as harmless and respectable. The trio is momentarily distracted by more church singing.

A knock at the door again initiates a virtually identical confrontation as in the white church version between the family, the police officers and the alleged rape victim. However, soon after Tom is taken out of the house by the arresting officers, another friend, Matilda Brown, rushes over to tell Sue about a growing mob's plan to lynch Tom. This time, Sue and Liza brainstorm with Matilda and they collectively decide that they must enlist the help of Miss Vilet, the daughter of a judge who Sue nursed as a child. Matilda volunteers to run the errand, and Bossie takes off with her. Sue and Liza audibly pray as they anxiously await Matilda and Bossie's return. Sue and Liza's dialogue is alternately broken up by church singing and prayers breaks. Feeling ill, Sue sits down and asks Liza to retrieve her bottle of camphor, a folk remedy used during bouts of nervousness.

Liza attends to Sue with oil as well as reassuring words about both Matilda and Tom's safe return. Matilda is then heard running toward them. Sue excitedly asks about Miss Vilet's response when Matilda breaks the bad news to them. It is too late. Tom is lynched. As Bossie approaches her crying, Sue collapses into a chair. Matilda and Liza try to revive her with camphor oil but to no avail. Sue is dead due to poor health and a heart attack. In both versions of Johnson's plays, Grandma Sue suffers a heart attack upon hearing of her innocent grandson's lynching. In this way, Johnson depicts the effects of lynching as harming more than just innocent young male victims; lynching also has an indirect effect of killing close family members who, due to white supremacy, are in poor health.

Johnson's two versions of *A Sunday Morning in the South* reveal much about the ways she appealed to respective audiences. In representing elderly black women as head of household, Stephens observes Johnson's focus on the specific ways lynching affected black women. Despite her death at the end of the plays, Sue Jones is heralded for her quick-thinking actions in trying to prevent her grandson's death. Stephens also praises Johnson's depiction of a black extended family which includes close family friends as part of its non-traditional makeup.[44] Despite her age and infirmity, Stephens holds up Sue Jones as an image characterized more accurately by her strong spirit and community ties rather than her weak body.

I echo Stephens' observations regarding Johnson's "communal sensibility," especially with regard to how Johnson's anti-lynching plays function within the black community into which they were written and (intended to be) performed. Johnson's depiction of an elderly black woman raising two adolescent boys is not necessarily ideal; however, the situation provides instruction to the actors who perform the play since, according to Timothy J. Wiles' reading of Aristotle, modern artist "moves the incidents out of the realm of the contingent and accidental . . . and orders them into a dramatic action to show how and why they occur, particularly connecting with the quality of men who perform them." Additionally, for black and white audiences alike, watching a grandmother die of a heart (break) attack evokes an affective response in them, effectively purifying them "by increasing their sensitivity."[45]

More pointedly, Johnson's representation of an elderly black woman caring for two black male children directly challenged "the Mammy myth," a pure figment of the white imagination popularized through Harriet Beecher Stowe's 1858 novel and the staged adaptations of the book that followed, also known as "Tom Plays." Mammy, a fictional image of black women, solely created "as the desired collaborator within white society: idealized by the master class, a trumped-up, not a triumphant, figure in the mythologizing of slavery," and according to Toni Morrison, an "enabler" of whiteness.[46] On the contrary, Sue is depicted as responsible and loving, even though her love may be tough. She provides for the young black boys a safe, structured environment in which they can express themselves both intellectually and emotionally. Unlike a Mammy figure, Sue does not derive her status based on her proximity to or influence with whites as she only refers to them as a desperate, last resort measure. She has real friends who help her when she needs it. Summarily, Sue in no way represents a stereotypical Mammy image for audiences of *A Sunday in the South's* white church version. Sue's onstage interactions with her grandsons and women friends do not reproduce white supremacist stereotype. On the contrary, Sue is humanized and rendered mortal.

For both black and white audiences, *A Sunday Morning in the South* clarifies several aspects of lynching performances, especially with regard to preliminary lynching performances such as "burnt cork crimes" and the unjust way the police coerce an ignorant young white woman into identifying an alleged black male rapist. Johnson also shone a light on certain aspects of lynching performances that can only be interrogated when dramatically staged, including the police's intrusion into the Jones household and the continuous disrespect of Sue by various white men she encounters. Johnson's portrayal of these details refers to blacks' inability to defend themselves whether verbally, through testimony, or through physical resistance. Even when Sue and Bossie's testimony is offered under oath, their alibis do nothing to thwart Tom's lynching. Additionally, when the black women come up with an idea to solicit an intervention from a reputable white man, their good idea goes untested due to both the disrespect shown to Sue by white men as well as the speed with which the mob carries out the lynching. Johnson presents these whiteness performance practices as symbolically equivalent, resulting in Sue's and Tom's respective deaths due to their precarious subjectivities as an elderly black woman and a young black man.

Specific appeals within the white and black versions include other details omitted in either one or the other play. For example, only in the black church version of *A Sunday Morning in the South* are we provided details about how Tom sustains his back injury while working for Mr. John. Tom and his grandmother openly discuss Mr. John's abuse and exploitation of Tom's labor by expecting him to lift a box too heavy for one man. Mr. John subjects Tom to treatment as a beast of burden, or as a horse, in the words of Sue, an allusion indicating that Tom is dehumanized, overworked and underpaid. Exploitation of Tom's labor is later echoed by Sue and Liza when they later reference a lynching of Zeb Brooks[47] who was killed as a result of a labor dispute. Although the reference is clear in the black version, the white version avoids mention of how Tom hurt his back or why he so was exhausted from work the day before.

Johnson's inclusion of a discussion between Sue and Tom about the exploitation of black men's labor in the play's black version reflects her consideration of a black audience who was subject to these conditions, but could not necessarily protest them or even discuss them publicly. Also, Johnson documents how an exploitation of labor and lynching worked hand in hand during Jim Crow modernity. Mr. John's exploitation of Tom's labor foregrounds how Jim Crow's intersecting mechanisms reworked and extended "previous structures of captivity and abjection through gendered capitalism" to make the New South possible.[48] Even though Tom and Grandma Sue are always, already vulnerable to "captivity and abjection" the two engage in a subversive conversation about Tom's working conditions in the same way a black audience engages in such discussions amongst themselves but not necessarily outside of the black community.

The white church version portrays Sue as healthy enough to run to the white church herself instead of having to send her friend and youngest grandson. In this way, I think Johnson presented a healthier version of Sue so as not to drag out the play or bother white audiences with Sue's personal details about which they little cared. Like the details of Tom's back injury, Sue's personal health concerns are shared with the black church community only.[49] Also, the encounter between Sue and Judge Manning provides one final opportunity to depict the disrespectful way white men interact with black women to devastating effects.

Conversely, Sue's poorer quality of health, as presented in the black church version, provided a chance for Johnson to express ambivalence regarding the way black church members treated Sue due to her physical condition. Instead of comforting her in her time of illness and pain, black church members ostracize Sue by making her feel ashamed of her condition. As a result, she stops attending Sunday worship services. Because of Johnson's repeated representation of such ambivalence toward God and the black church in other plays,[50] Johnson's dramatics may indicate "proximity to . . . philosophical movements" demonstrating a "larger connection to the general trends of modernism."[51] I would argue that Sue's ostracism by the black church sets Johnson up to re-imagine the function of the church in the community. When Sue and Liza stay home from church, instead listening to gospel hymns through an open window, Johnson promotes "the idea of art as religion and as a way of life," an idea that "was not uncommon among the avant-garde movements of the time."[52] Instead of depicting the black church as a centerpiece of Sue's life, gospel hymns as sung by the choir are utilized as a source of Sue's peace and comfort in her final moments. As such, Johnson foregrounds the art of the black church, as opposed to the gospel, as Sue's religion, even as the choir's singing and Liza's prayers serve as her last rites before she collapses and dies.

Both the black church version and the white church version of *A Sunday in the South* include Johnson's handwritten arrangements of traditional spirituals and hymns to accompany the plays. Johnson incorporates specific songs according to the race-based version of the play. In keeping with a white affinity for an emerging popular culture tradition, Johnson arranges Antonin Dvorak's Symphony no. 9 for use in the white church version, as aforementioned. Johnson's use of this song contrasts with minstrelsy's exploitation and mocking of black music forms. Instead of repeating a use of black spirituals to misrepresent black people's images, Dvorak used the pieces as inspiration to create a "great and noble" composition.[53] Not only does Johnson incorporate Symphony no. 9 as a white music element, but she uses the composition to model for white audiences how to respectfully interact with black cultural traditions.

The gospel hymns incorporated in the black church version represent traditional gospel hymns that were not necessarily written by black composers yet comprise black church standards with which the audience would easily recognize and sing. In this way, the black church version of *A Sunday in the South* performs affectively, facilitating *communitas* through a call and response patterning between the text and the audience.

Using Chamber Theatre technique to examine white households in "Saving White Face"

Finally, it is through examining lynching dramas in white domestic environs using Chamber Theatre technique that lynching's "motivation at the moment of action"[54] is illuminated, thus achieving catharsis as modern theatre. This clarification is accomplished through the use of Chamber Theatre techniques which are dedicated

> to the proposition that the ideal literary experience is one which the simultaneity of the drama, representing the illusion of actuality (that is, social and psychological realism), may be profitably combined with the novel's narrative privilege of examining human motivation at the moment of action.[55]

Even further, although Kirk Fuoss outlines components of a lynching performance complex in "Lynching Performances, Theaters of Violence," he fails to specifically identify white domestic environments as primary sites of preliminary lynching performances. However, lynching dramas set in white homes illuminate these environments' functioning as such, while also undermining "the coherence of categories like the *personal* and the *political*"[56] as well as the *public* and the *private*. Lynching plays set in white households reveal lynching performances as not only intertwined with Southern political activity but as cognate, if not synonymous performances.

"Saving White Face" depicts several incidents of domestic violence as preliminary lynching performance, such as in the following scene which occurs soon after Lily has an indirect encounter with a young black boy in the pool hall owned by her husband Floyd, yet frequented by local black laborers:

> (Lily moves to center stage where there is a bench or two chairs where she is waiting for Floyd. A Patsy Cline song begins to play, "I Fall to Pieces." She is lost in the song; and does not see or hear Floyd approach from stage right. He is angry.)
>
> *Ida:* The slap caught her by surprise; it was heavy handed and so full of meanness and rage she couldn't even cry. Lily was stunned. Floyd had hit her before, but she always knew when the blow coming.

"Saving White Face's" depiction of domestic violence in the Cox household prefigures the lynching that occurs soon afterward. As such, domestic violence functions as preliminary lynching performance since the violence is repeated (with variation) soon afterwards. Floyd might be thought to be "warming up" for his later actions or could be said to be (symbolically) treating Lily like he knows he will later be expected to treat his African American victim. In this way, lynching dramas prove to be crucial in unmasking how domestic violence taking place within white homes is found to function as precursors to lynchings occurring outside the homes later. Lynching performances are now more broadly understood as acts of domestic terrorism that begin within the white household.

Mirroring modern Lily

"Saving White Face" illustrates "Ida's" full integration into lynching culture as she and Lily Cox "mirror" one another. Chamber Theatre, Breen observes, "may take advantage of a mirror convention to express an objective description of a character even though a mirror is not physically present in the scene."[57] In "Saving White Face's" first scene, before any of the dialogue begins, Lily joins Ida at center stage where they simultaneously recite Brooks' poetry while performing stylized movements as if applying makeup:

Ida: From the first it had been like a Ballad.
        It had the beat inevitable. It had the blood.
        A wildness cut up, and tied in little bunches,
        Like the four-line stanzas of the ballads she had never quite Understood-the ballads they had set her to, in school.
Lily: Herself: the milk white maid, the "maid mild"
        Of the ballad. Pursued
        By the Dark Villain. Rescued by the Fine Prince. The Happiness-Ever-After.

In these opening lines, Brooks' poem directly references "the lynching story" as a "Ballad," thereby evoking Romanticism, or an idealized narrative.[58] Brooks also made direct reference to actual lynching ballads, a genre within a "folk culture of lynching" reminding us of lynching's makeup as,

> a cultural text made up of many elements operating on different levels. The event sequence, like the other elements, is a stylized action laden with meaning which is intended to convey a message to various audiences. This metaphor of the lynching as a text, that is, of many different elements each contributing to the

propagation of messages, allows us to see the cultural expressions about lynching, whether in novels, newspapers, or ballads, as a part of the lynching.[59]

In "Saving White Face," Brooks' poem functions as black feminist criticism of "the lynching story," especially with regard to white female subjects' misrepresentation as "innocent victims." As observed by Schechter, Ida B. Wells-Barnett's *Southern Horrors* first critiques white women's images: "Well's reports of consensual and sometimes illicit sexual contact between white women and black men and of white women's role in abetting mobs undermined the assumption of white women's moral purity used to justify lynching."[60] "Saving White Face" repositions Lily's marginal, passive role as "victim" in "the lynching story" to center stage, revealing her anxieties, internal conflicts and search for self- knowledge.[61] According to Dieckmann, Lily presents as an "internally alienated modern self"[62] through whom an audience can "think critically about, rather than identify with, the situation presented."[63] Black feminist Chamber Theatre technique re-presents Lily's "split subjectivity"[64] in "the lynching story," as subject/object, illuminating her as both lyncher and "lynchee."

"Saving White Face" depicts how Lily's lack of self-reflexivity and desires perpetuate a lynching nightmare. We learn that it is Lily's willingness to literally and figuratively "buy into" modern concepts of femininity, dependence and family perpetuated by "the lynching story" that helps justify her husband's and in-laws' actions, as depicted in an early scene:

Lily: Lily pressed her breasts into Floyd's bare back. She wanted him to wake up feeling the tips of her nipples against his skin.

Ida: She smiled thinking how she could make him want her, remembering the times he even begged. She thought:

Lily: If I can get him to give me three dollars, I'll get me another Rio Red lipstick; ain't had a lipstick in going on three months. I might can buy me some Evening in Paris and a scarf too. And maybe some rose colored nail polish.

Ida: She calmed herself because the trick was to wake Floyd softly . . . to make it seem coincidental that the front of her nightgown was undone, her breasts exposed. Wanting her had to be his idea, he didn't like it the other way around.

Lily: Floyd said only whores acted that way.

Lily's desire to consume "a Rio Red lipstick, Evening in Paris perfume, a scarf and rose colored nail polish" can be traced to a dialectic established at the turn of the century. Hale and Wallace outline spectacle lynching as a (literal) product of consumer culture as well as a cognate of turn of the twentieth-century world fairs and expositions, respectively. Hale explains lynching's tie to consumption, a hallmark of the modern era:

> In a grisly dialectic, then, consumer culture created spectacle lynchings, and spectacle lynchings became a southern way of enabling the spread of consumption as a white privilege. The violence both helped create a white consuming public and the structure of segregation where consumption could take place without threatening white supremacy.[65]

Peggy Phelan' s *Unmarked* (1996) further explains Floyd's failure to please his wife (both materially and sexually) as indicative of the couple's failure to *mirror* each other since, "a failure to secure self-seeing (that) leads to the imagination of annihilation and castration,"[66] a fantasy that is later projected onto a young black lynching victim. Therefore, it is Lily's unmet desires that are the touchtone of this scene and can be understood to "key" or set up a "culturally conventionalized metacommunicative frame"[67] in "Saving White Face." According to Bauman, "The essential task in the ethnography of performance is to determine *the culture-specific constellations of communicative means that serve to key performance in particular communities.*"[68] "Saving White Face" finds Lily's seduction of Floyd as a means of participating in whiteness consumer culture to "key" its lynching performance.

In direct contrast to Lily's inability to see herself in Floyd, Lily achieves reflexivity in "Saving White Face" by being mirrored by Ida. Instead of through the use of an actual mirror, Ida functions as Lily's mirror. Ida mirrors Lily, dramatizing Lily's conflicting selves – her object "self" as well as her subject "self." Ida reflects Lily in a way that Floyd cannot. Since their onstage relationship is in no way competitive, "Ida" is not subject to repercussions from Lily because of it. Ida and Lily's onstage performance counters those offstage in which interests of middle-class white women overshadow black women's subjectivity. Finally, Ida's mirroring Lily is a means by which "Saving White Face" performs Dieckmann's link between historicization and alienation.[69] Ida represents a historical past that when linked with Lily's (modern) alienation "facilitate(s) transformation."[70] "Saving White Face" transforms "the lynching story" from a whiteness narrative masking white supremacy into a black feminist performance.

Not only does Ida mirror Lily, but Lily also performs as Ida's mirror. In this way, Ida and Lily perform as each other's double, which is a provocative exploration of their relationship within lynching culture as a black woman and a white woman. First, it is through Lily's mirroring that a representation of black women as a more likely victim of rape/lynching becomes clear. In other words, Lily[71] mirrors Ida to illuminate rape and murder from which Ida, as a black woman, cannot be protected. Unlike offstage where Lily's uncritical, whiteness performance (re)produces black women's rape/lynching, in "Saving White Face" Lily helps to foreground these practices which counteracts "the lynching story's" repression of this truth.

Ida and Lily also mirror an offstage dynamic between black and white American women who worked respectively as anti-lynching activists and playwrights. Not only does Ida represent Ida's B. Wells-Barnett's launch of anti-lynching/rape activism, but Lily, when mirrored by Ida, might be thought to reflect the possibilities of (middle class) white women like Jessie Daniel Ames (1883–1972). Through the Association of Southern Women for the Prevention of Lynching (ASWPL), Ames targeted white audiences using rhetorical strategies that differed sharply from those of African American anti-lynching activists.[72] Although Ames believed that African Americans could do little to deter lynching themselves, she delivered speeches arguing against the whiteness performance practice as well as, through the ASWPL, sponsored lynching playwriting contests, as will be again discussed in Chapter 3. Crystal N. Feimster also represents such a mirroring of black/white woman anti-rape/lynching activism in *Southern Horrors* (2009) in which she juxtaposes Wells-Barnett's anti-rape activism to that of Rebecca Latimore Felton (1835–1930).[73]

In addition to anti-lynching/rape activism, Ida and Lily also represent black and white women as anti-lynching dramatists about whom Judith Stephen cogently observes:

> Anti-lynching ideology clearly created a common aesthetic ground for black and white women playwrights, which can be recognized in the reciprocity of ideas and frequent repetitions of dramatic techniques chosen to represent the brutality and injustice of lynching. These plays are complementary and reciprocal,

both womanist and feminist, in that they reflect commonalities and differences between and among black and white women.[74]

Finally, both Ida and Lily perform on "a common aesthetic ground," in a blueswoman aesthetic, although each performs her respective version. One way "Saving White Face" represents Lily's blues is through an inclusion of Patsy Cline's song "I Fall to Pieces." The song track plays in the background as Floyd violently smacks Lily upon hearing of her pool hall encounter with the young, black boy. "Saving White's Face's" mirroring of a white blueswoman aesthetic reflects a black feminist "producerly orientation,"[75] according to Dieckmann. "Saving White Face" performs as "embodied poststructuralist theory,"[76] reflecting black blueswomen tradition as a black feminism also performed by white women. Blueswomen performance in "Saving White Face" represents a radical, black feminist practice useful to all oppressed women, no matter their race or class.

Like anti-lynching plays taking place in black domestic environments, anti-lynching plays taking place in white domestic environments are found to clarify lynching performances, especially by staging white households as sites of preliminary and embedded lynching performances as well as "unmasking" non-verbal and micro-aggressive whiteness communicative practices operating within "the lynching complex." Close readings of anti-lynching plays taking place in white households reveal how duping, scapegoating and con games play integral roles in lynching performance practice as well. White woman's verbal performances as active and passive bearers of a whiteness performance tradition, as well as intracultural performances based on (desire) for consumerism reflect an image of white women contrary to the way she is portrayed in "the lynching story." Lynching drama depicts white women not as helpless victims in need of rescue from black men; if anything, she needs to be rescued from brutish white men. Better yet, as a critical thinker, the white woman subject is presented with the possibility of leaving the proverbial white household in which lynching performances are embedded to create a new, non-normative image of white womanhood.

Notes

1 Perkins and Stephens, *Strange Fruit*, 5.
2 Turner, *From Ritual to Theatre*, 28.

3 Frances Early, "Whiteness and Political Purpose in 'The Noose,' an Antilynching Play by Tracy Mygatt," *Women's History Review* 11, no. 1 (2002), 27.

4 See Mitchell, *Living With Lynching*; and Anna Jo Paul, *Strange Fruit: An Examination and Comparison of Themes in Anti-Lynching Dramas of Black and White Women Authors of the Early Twentieth Century (1916–1936)*, Ph.D. dissertation, University of Louisville, 2015.

5 Paul, *Strange Fruit*, VII.

6 Kirk Fuoss, "Lynching Performances, Theatre of Violence," *Text and Performance Quarterly* 19, no. 1 (January 1999), 9.

7 Early, "Whiteness and Political Purpose in 'The Noose'," 7.

8 Perkins and Stephens, *Strange Fruit*, 27.

9 See Jessie Daniel Ames, *Revolt Against Chivalry: Jessie Daniel Ames and the Women's Campaign Against Chivalry* (New York, NY: Columbia University Press, 1979).

10 Early, "Whiteness and Political Purpose in 'The Noose'," 28.

11 Lynn Dumenil, *The Second Line of Defense: American Women and World War I* (Chapel Hill, NC: University of North Carolina Press, 2017), 26.

12 Ibid.

13 Early, "Whiteness and Political Purpose in 'The Noose'," 30.

14 "The White Brute" is published in Mary Ovington and Ralph E. Luker (eds.), *Black and White Sat Down Together: The Reminisces of an NAACP Founder* (New York, NY: Feminist Press at City University of New York, 1995), 137–46.

15 Elaine Scarry, *The Body in Pain: The Making and Unmaking of the World* (New York, NY: Oxford University Press, 1985), 61.

16 Ibid.

17 Early, "Whiteness and Political Purpose in 'The Noose'," 33.

18 Ibid, 50.

19 Ibid, 34.

20 Ibid.

21 Ibid, 44.

22 Ibid, 39.

23 Haley, *No Mercy Here*, 9.

24 Perkins and Stephens, *Strange Fruit*, 93.

25 Ibid, 97.

26 Fuoss, "Lynching Performances," 11.

27 Bauman, *Verbal Art as Performance*, 13.

28 The Howard Players was officially established in 1919, a year before her graduation. May Miller's coming of age at Howard occurred at the exact moment in which black intellectuals and artists were considering the role of drama in combatting misrepresentation, appropriation and devaluation of black culture and images.

29 Personal Diary, Box 8, Folder 1, "February 17, 1934," May Miller Papers 1909–1990, Stuart A. Rose Manuscript, Archives and Rare Book Library, Emory University Libraries.

30 Richardson and Miller, *Negro History in Thirteen Plays*.

31 Kathy Perkins and Judith L. Stephens, "May Miller," in *Strange Fruit: Plays on Lynching by American Women* (Bloomington, IN: Indiana University Press, 1998), 175-76.

32   S. Randolph Edmonds to Mae (sic) Miller, Box 1, Folder "1930," May Miller Papers 1909–1990, Stuart A. Rose Manuscript, Archives and Rare Book Library, Emory University Libraries.

33   Ibid, 177.

34   Ibid, 179.

35   Mary Russo, "Female Grotesques: Carnival and Theory," in Teresa de Lauretis (ed.), *Feminist Studies/Critical Studies* (London: Palgrave Macmillan, 1986), 218.

36   Ibid.

37   Perkins and Stephens, *Strange Fruit*, 188.

38   Ibid, 183.

39   Mary Turner, 19, was eight months pregnant and the mother of two when she was lynched in 1918 for protesting her husband's murder. Turner's lynching has not been directly represented in a lynching play although I would argue that Miller alludes to the incident in *Nails and Thorns*, inverting Turner's subjectivity with that of Gladys.

40   Perkins and Stephens, *Strange Fruit*, 175.

41   Alain Locke and Thomas Montgomery Gregory (eds.), *Plays of Negro Life* (Westport, CT: Negro Universities Press, 1970), 215–33.

42   Fuoss, "Lynching Performances," 14–15.

43   See Mitchell-Kernan, "Signifying," 310–28.

44   Stephens, *The Plays of Georgia Douglas Johnson*, 35.

45   Timothy J. Wiles, *The Theatre Event: Modern Theories of Performance* (Chicago, IL: University of Chicago Press, 1980), 5.

46   See Judith Williams, "Uncle Tom's Women," in Harry Elam and David Krasner (eds.), *African American Theatre and Performance History* (New York, NY: Oxford University Press, 2001), 19–39 in which Williams discusses how Tom plays after Uncle Tom's Cabin was published established stereotype of Topsy, the tragic mulatto and Mammy.

47   I could find no historical incident in which a "Zeb Brooks" is lynched; however, disputes between laborers and employers were rampant in this era as referenced by other lynchings including that of Sam Hosea (1899) to which Johnson refers in *Safe*.

48   Haley, *No Mercy Here*, 3.

49   It is possible Johnson could refer to a range of practices related to the medical exploitation of blacks, from overcharging for medical services up to and including black bodies' subjugation to Western medical experimentation.

50   In *Safe*, Liza questions God, expressing her preference for a girl over a boy. It can even be argued that she plays God in committing infanticide as soon as her healthy baby boy is born.

51   Wiles, *The Theatre Event*, 23. Although no record exists, I am here tying Johnson's writing to dramatic criticism and acting methods of Russian theatre practitioner Constantin Stanislavski (1863–1938) who was also considered a modern era reformer of drama.

52   Ibid, 34. By juxtaposing Johnson's anti-lynching playwriting to that of Stanislavski I mean to reinforce the genre's identity as an avant-garde theatre movement, among others.

53   Joseph Horowitz, "New World Symphony and Discord," *Chronicle of Higher Education* 54, no. 18 (January 11, 2008), B18-B19.

54   Breen, *Chamber Theatre*, 4.

55 Ibid, 5.
56 Blocker, *Where Is Ana Mendieta?* 24.
57 Breen, *Chamber Theatre*, 11.
58 For a more detailed discussion of Romance in American literature, see Toni Morrison's *Playing in the Dark: Whiteness and the Literary Imagination* (New York, NY: Random House, 1992).
59 Bruce Baker, "North Carolina Lynching Ballads," in W. Fitzhugh Brundage (ed.), *Under Sentence of Death: Lynching in the South* (Chapel Hill, NC: University of North Carolina Press, 1997), 220–21.
60 Schechter, "Unsettled Business," 293.
61 Breen, *Chamber Theatre*, 7.
62 Dieckmann, "Toward a Feminist Chamber," 47.
63 Ibid, 46.
64 Ibid, 47.
65 Hale, *Making Whiteness*, 205–6.
66 Phelan, *Unmarked*, 20.
67 Bauman, *Verbal Art as Performance*, 15.
68 Ibid, 22.
69 Dieckmann, "Toward a Feminist Chamber," 47.
70 Ibid.
71 Lily is subject to domestic violence and unsatisfying/unwanted sex in "Saving White Face" that I would argue effectively mirrors the rape and lynching of black women.
72 See Jacquelyn Dowd Hall's *Revolt Against Chivalry: Jessie Daniel Ames and the Women's Campaign Against Lynching* (New York, NY: Columbia University Press, 1979).
73 See Feimster, *Southern Horrors*.
74 Perkins and Stephens, *Strange Fruit*, 11.
75 Dieckmann, "Toward a Feminist Chamber," 52.
76 Ibid, 47.

Bibliography

Baker, Bruce. 1997. "North Carolina Lynching Ballads." In *Under Sentence of Death: Lynching in the South*, edited by W. Fitzhugh Brundage, 219–46. Chapel Hill, NC: University of North Carolina Press.

Bauman, Richard. 1977. *Verbal Art as Performance*. Prospect Heights, IL: Waveland Press.

Blocker, Jane. 1999. *Where Is Ana Mendieta: Identity, Performance and Exile*. Durham, NC: Duke University Press.

Breen, Robert S. 1978. *Chamber Theatre*. Englewood Cliffs, NJ: Prentice-Hall.

Dieckmann, Lara E. 1999. "Towards a Feminist Chamber Theatre Method." *Text and Performance Quarterly* 19: 38–56.

Dumenil, Lynn. 2017. *The Second Line of Defense: American Women and World War I*. Chapel Hill, NC: University of North Carolina Press.

Early, Frances. 2002. "Whiteness and Politcal Purpose in 'The Noose,' an Antilynching Play by Tracy Mygatt." *Women's History Review* 11, no. 1: 27–48.

Feimster, Nicole. 2009. *Southern Horrors: Women and Politics of Rape and Lynching.* Cambridge, MA: Harvard University Press.

Fuoss, Kirk. 1999. "Lynching Performances, Theatres of Violence." *Text and Performance Quarterly*: 1–37.

Haley, Sarah. 2016. *No Mercy Here: Gender, Punishment and Making of Jim Crow Modernity.* Chapel Hill, NC: University of North Carolina Press.

Hall, Jacqueline Dowd. 1979. *Revolt Against Chivalry: Jessie Daniel Ames and the Women's Campaign Against Chivalry.* New York, NY: Columbia University Press.

Horowitz, Joseph. 2008. "New World Symphony and Discord." *Chronicle of Higher Education*: B18-B19. Accessed May 21, 2019. http://search.ebscohost.com/login. aspx?direct=true&db=mzh&AN=2008300719&site=eds-live&scope=site.

"May Miller Papers." 1909–1990. *Stuart A. Rose Manuscript.* Atlanta, GA: Archives and Rare Book Library, Emory University.

Mitchell, Koritha. 2011. *Living With Lynching: African American Lynching Plays, Performance and Citizenship, 1830–1930.* Urbana, IL: University of Illinois Press.

Mitchell-Kernan, Claudia. 1990. "Signifying." In *Mother Wit from the Laughing Barrel: Readings in the Interpretation of Afro-American Folklore*, edited by Alan Dundes, 310–28. Jackson, MS: University of Mississippi Press.

Morrison, Toni. 1993. *Playing in the Dark: Whiteness in the Literary Imagination.* New York, NY: Vintage Books.

Ovington, Mary. 1995. "The White Brute." In *Black and White Sat Down Together: The Reminisces of an NAACP Founder*, edited by Mary White Ovington and Ralph E. Luker, 137–46. New York, NY: Feminist Press at The City University of New York.

Perkins, Kathy A., and Judith L. Stephens. 1998. *Strange Fruit: Plays on Lynching by American Women.* Bloomington, IN: Indiana University Press.

Richardson, Willis, and May Miller. 1935. *Negro History in Thirteen Plays.* Washington, DC: The Associated Publishers, Inc.

Rogers Jr., John William. 1970. "Judge Lynch." In *Plays of Negro Life*, edited by Alain Locke and Thomas Montgomery Gregory, 215–33. Westport, CT: Negro Universities Press.

Russo, Mary. 1986. "Female Grotesques: Carnival and Theory." In *Feminist Studies/Critical Studies*, edited by Teresa de Lauretis, 213–29. London: Palgrave Macmillan.

Scarry, Elaine. 1985. *The Body in Pain: The Making and Unmaking of the World.* New York, NY: Oxford University Press.

Schechter, Patricia. 1997. "Unsettled Business: Ida B. Wells Against Lynching or, How Antilynching Got Its Gender." In *Under Sentence of Death: Lynching in the South*, edited by W. Fitzhugh Brundage, 293–313. Chapel Hill, NC: University of North Carolina Press.

Stephens, Judith L. 2006. *The Plays of Georgia Douglas Johnson: From the Negro Renaissance to the Civil Rights Movement.* Urbana-Champaign, IL: University of Illinois Press.

Wiles, Timothy J. 1980. *The Theatre Event: Modern Theories of Performance*. Chicago, IL: University of Chicago Press.

Williams, Judith. 2001. "Uncle Tom's Women." In *African American Theatre and Performance History*, edited by Harry Elam and David Krasner, 19–39. New York, NY: Oxford University Press.

Chapter 3

Sketches from a black feminist professor's notebook

Staging lynching plays at a Historically Black College and University (HBCU) in the South

Fort Valley State University's Joseph Adkins Players (JAP) first staged "Saving White Face," a contemporary lynching play, on April 12, 2012,[1] less than two months after George Zimmerman, 28, shot and killed 17-year-old Trayvon Martin, a Miami, Florida, native. Staging "Saving White Face" functioned as an artist response to Martin's murder with a production goal of contesting Zimmerman's version of events in which he claimed to have killed Martin in self-defense. Zimmerman, an unofficial "neighborhood watchman," confronted Martin as he walked home from a nearby convenience store to a Sanford, Florida, condominium complex where he lived with his father. An altercation ensued, which resulted in Martin's death. Contrary to Zimmerman's version of events and even his eventual acquittal, "Saving White Face" theorized Martin's murder as a whiteness cultural performance, specifically as lynching performance. "Saving White Face" examined Martin's murder as a "performance saturated event," identifying the ways the murder conformed to "the lynching cycle," including "preliminary, embedded and subsequent performances."[2] As such, "Saving White Face" functioned to clarify Martin's murder as an act of American injustice that infringed upon Martin's civil rights, especially with regard to Zimmerman's arrest and prosecution.[3]

As a lynching play, "Saving White Face" also performed as social protest, reflecting a tradition of African American theatre practitioners who "use theatre as a means[4] of protest and revolt in order to change black lives and fight oppressive conditions." Fort Valley State University's Joseph Adkins Players student drama group effectively protested the institutionalized racism and state sanctioned violence that delayed Zimmerman's arrest for 45 days and eventually acquitted him. The JAP student drama group staged "Saving White Face" to publically protest Martin's murder in the same way as marchers who flooded American streets all over the country using Skittles and hoodies to underscore the senselessness of Martin's death. Such protest performances against Martin's murder eventually resulted in a movement known as #blacklivesmatter.[5]

Although a comprehensive archive does not exist, drama clubs and departments at Historically Black College and Universities (HBCUs) such as FVSU must ostensibly be considered as primary outlets for social protest performances, especially lynching plays, since the plays did not enjoy mainstream theatre production. In fact Angelina Weld Grimke's *Rachel*, "the first black authored, nonmusical drama"[6] ever produced for a black audience by the Washington, D.C., chapter of the NAACP, was staged at the Myrtilla Miner Normal School for Colored Girls, an institution established by the educator and abolitionist for black girls.[7] In *Colored No More: Reinventing Black Womanhood in Washington* (2017), Treva Lindsey observes the centrality of Washington, D.C.'s formal "black educational institutions such as Shaw Junior High, M Street High School and Howard University"[8] to the development of plays written by black authors at institutions where they taught, worked together as colleagues and directed new plays. Lindsey also examines the significance of informal or non-traditional black art institutions like the home of Georgia Douglas Johnson, also known as the S Street Salon, to the development of a community of black women playwrights emerging in the 1910s and 1920s, from where many lynching plays emerged.

Although little archival evidence is located, Ann Seymour Link's lynching drama *Lawd, Does You Undahstan?* (1936), which was awarded the Association of Southern Women in the Prevention of Lynching's (ASWPL) second prize, was staged at an HBCU in Augusta, Georgia, Paine College. Even further, in a 1936 letter addressed to "Miss Mae Miller" from S. Randolph Edmonds, the Dillard University theatre professor expresses his regret for Miller's third place finish in the (same contest as Link) ASWPL playwriting contest as well as confirmation of a five dollar royalty payment for a production of her historical play, *Harry Tubman* (sic). Also, Edmonds expression his plans to stage Miller's 1933 lynching play, *Nails and Thorns*.[9] As black feminist cultural production, lynching plays were not often produced on mainstream stages or popularly enjoyed by audiences, a scant record exists of the genre's production at black educational institutions where a Negro Little Theatre community emerged among a collective of early black theatre dramatists and practitioners.

The Negro Little Theatre Movement: HBCU's and lynching plays

In a 1949 journal article entitled "The Negro Little Theatre Movement," S. Randolph Edmonds surveys the history of black theatre in America, dividing the institution's development into three eras: 1865–1920; the 1920s; and the Negro Little Theatre Movement after the 1920s. According to Edmonds, the development of a national black (nee Negro) program was necessary in ensuring a full range of opportunities and inclusion for black theatre practitioners as well as a commitment to an accurate representation of black people on stage. After passing through amateur and entertainment phases, which are especially characterized by an absence of black playwrights as well as a preponderance of musicals and "farcical"[10] shows, Edmonds describes a post-1920 turn to a Little Theatre Movement which took place in communities and at colleges around the country. He especially focuses on dramatics practiced at Historically Black Colleges and Universities (HBCUs), an arena to which he contributed significantly. In founding the Negro Inter-Collegiate Drama Association on March 7, 1930,[11] Edmonds used an "organizational approach" which is defined as "drama groups in many localities working together as a unit to advance the same type of program."[12] Community theatres who used an organizational approach include the America Negro Theatre and W.E.B. Du Bois' Krigwa Little Theater Movement with branches located in most major cities throughout the country. An organizational model stands in contrast to "the individualistic approach" of a College Little Theatre Movement which was first exemplified by the Howard Players[13] who, between 1917 and 1920, represented the first "laboratory where young Negroes might receive dramatic training."[14] Included in an audacious agenda for the drama group were plays written about black life. The Howard Players produced many successful plays about black life; however, the Howard Players did not stage any lynching plays. As the first directors of the Howard Players, Alain Locke and T. Montgomery Gregory did not include lynching plays in their dramatic repertoire. Such a limitation seems in keeping with Locke's particular determination to break from "old" Negro images, including folklore and images stereotyping blacks as weak or backwards. Through the Howard Players, Locke sought to advance an image of a "New Negro," a modern figure who "welcomes the new scientific rather than the old sentimental interest."[15] Locke's exclusion of lynching plays reflects his criticism of the blues/gospel aesthetic of the plays, as well as a rejection of the images of grieving women and black vernacular language. Consequently, the Howard Players' exclusion of lynching plays from its dramatic production repertoire can be understood as a(nother) contributing factor to the dramatic genre's suppression.

In any case, the high profile success enjoyed by the Howard Players inspired the formation of drama clubs at other HBCUs including: "Atlanta University, Morgan College, Hampton Institute, Tuskegee Institute, Tougaloo College, Tennessee State College, Virginia State College, Fisk University, Shaw University and many others."[16] However, Edmonds concludes, due to their individualistic approaches, these programs were unable to "establish a permanent and far reaching Little Theatre Movement."[17]

In response to this dilemma, Edmonds moved to Dillard University where he established the Southern Association of Dramatic and Speech Arts on March 27, 1936, as the first of its kind in the Deep South. Subsequently, dramatic activity increased at these institutions as well as among high schools throughout the South. Edmonds cites the organizational aims of these newly created entities as follows:

> To encourage the study of drama in the member institutions by introducing courses, departments and workshops; to exchange plays and productions; to encourage the writing of plays based on Negro life and experience; to introduce world drama to the students through classroom study and productions; to hold professional meetings; to present festivals and tournaments; and to contribute towards building a National Negro Theatre as a significant aspect of American and world drama.[18]

As such, the Southern Association of Dramatic and Speech Arts (now known as the National Association of Dramatic and Speech Arts, or NADSA) reflected not only a quantitative stimulation in Negro (black) theatre but a qualitative improvement as well, since a number of directors of these new programs possessed doctorate degrees as well "the best technical training."[19] Among the number of highly trained progeny emerging under his influence, Edmonds included Joseph Adkins who went on to found a drama club at Fort

Valley State University and for whom the student drama club is now named.

A brief overview of theatre at Fort Valley State University

Joseph Adkins established the Fort Valley State College Players Guild in the late 1940s.[20] Adkins was a foremost student of the aforementioned S. Randolph Edmonds who is considered a "major influence" of black theatre in the South. In addition to founding Dillard University's Speech and Drama department which was the first to offer blacks course credit toward earning a degree in theatre, Edmonds, wrote 49 plays, chaired two other theatre departments and founded the National Association of Dramatic and Speech Arts (NADSA).[21] Edmonds' progeny, Joseph Adkins, directed Fort Valley's student drama group through the 1960s. Adkins served as NADSA's executive secretary for many years and was well known for producing one-acts that his students performed at SADSA's and NADSA's national festivals.[22] Some of these titles include George A. Towns' *The Share-croppers* (1941), *The Valiant* (1941), *Manikin and Minikin* (1949), *Special Guest* (1950), *Play Me No Carols* (1951), *Mooncalf Mugford* (1953), *The Other One* (1954), *Thirst* (1957) and *Patterns* (1958).[23]

Under the direction of Dr. Virgie Harris (retired), a Distinguished Professor of Speech and Drama, JAP was intermittently active in NADSA through the years 1983 to 1986 and then from 1989 to 2006. In fact, Dr. Harris actively contributed to the organization as an editor of its magazine publication as well as an organization board member. The trophy case in FVSU's Founders Hall prominently displays dozens of awards, making JAP's dramatic activity in NADSA undeniable. In the same tradition as the Negro Little Theatre movement, JAP continues to regularly produce plays and pageants that both provide performance-based training to its students as well as serve the HBCU community. In fact, due, in part, to the group's level of productivity, Fort Valley State University's Department of Visual and Performing Arts expanded its course offerings to introduce a degree concentration in Theatre and Performance Studies between 2015 and 2016.

As part of an emerging theatre and performance studies curriculum focused upon both theatre's aesthetics as well as its use as communication tool, the JAP drama club staged a lynching play series from 2012–2014. The series proceeded as a performance-based response to (collective) instances of vigilante terrorism and police brutality as well as, as an outgrowth of research conducted by this writer. In this chapter, I will document the series especially with regard to its performance as an extension of a historical Black Little Theater movement, establishment/recovery of the genre and staging black feminist theory/pedagogy in the United States' Middle Georgia region. Additionally, this chapter draws upon Anna Julia Cooper's dramatic theory and criticism as articulated in *A Voice From the South* (1892) and *Sketches from a Teacher's Notebook* (1923?). In doing so, FVSU's lynching play series is observed as black feminist performance, pedagogy and praxis.

Despite a lack of resources, often due to high turnover in administration,[24] theatre programs at HBCUs continue to train (primarily) black students for graduate school as well as professional careers in theatre, television and film. In fact, theatre programs at HBCUs are found to be vital to the well-being of the educational institutions themselves since they raise the profile of the schools. Theatre programs at HBCUs are also central to black theatre as a whole since, unlike PWIs, HBCUs consistently offer its black students major roles and can provide a curriculum geared to them as black theatre practitioners. Fort Valley State University (FVSU)'s Joseph Adkins Players student drama club offers its students opportunities to study black theatre and performance which includes an examination of the history and development of the discipline and the part JAP plays in it.

FVSU and black feminist performance in Middle Georgia

Fort Valley State University (FVSU) is located in the town of Fort Valley (population 9,815) which is about 100 miles south of Atlanta and 25 miles south of Macon, situating the town, geographically, at the heart of Georgia. Fort Valley serves as county seat of Peach County, Georgia, which was once known as "Peach Capital of the World."[25] FVSU enrolls approximately 3,000 students and is most known for its agriculture-based, veterinary technical academic programs as well as a nationally recognized Cooperative Development Energy Program. Established in 1895 as Fort Valley High and Industrial School, an interracial group of 15 men, which included three former slaves, chartered the school. Significantly, upon its restructuring as a four-year college in 1939, Dr. Horace Mann Bond, a University of Chicago trained educator and activist, was selected to serve at the institution's first president. Dr. Bond's son Julian went on to follow in his father's footsteps as a civil rights advocate by "becoming a founder of the Student Nonviolent Coordinating Committee, a Georgia state legislator, president of the Southern Poverty Law Center and chairman of the NAACP."[26]

Other noteworthy towns in the region include Eatonton, Georgia, hometown to Pulitzer Prize winner author Alice Walker who, throughout her fiction and poetry, documented cultural history, especially post-Emancipation, brown-skinned black women. Walker's oeuvre undoubtedly depicts stories encompassing residents of the town of Fort Valley, which is located about 70 miles southwest of Eatonton. Most significantly, Walker documents an early phase of institutionalized violence against black women in Georgia in her Pulitzer prize-winning novel, *The Color Purple* (1982), which includes a spectrum of violence occurring in the domestic realms of their homes and extending to violence sanctioned by the state through prisons. Through the image of the character Sophia, who was memorably portrayed by Oprah Winfrey[27] in the 1984 film version of the novel, Walker depicts "the mutually constitutive role of race and gender in constructing social positions, technologies of violence, understanding of the social order and the construction and application of the law,"[28] in the post-Reconstruction South. After leaving her husband for trying to "beat her into submission," Sophia is imprisoned for retaliating against the town mayor who has just slapped her after she refuses his wife's offer to work as her personal maid. In her award winning study, *No Mercy Here: Gender Punishment and the Making of Jim Crow Modernity* (2016), historian Sarah Haley contextualizes a "staggering" history of violence against black women that was instrumental in the making of the New South. In her examination of the American carceral system in a post-Reconstruction era, Haley cites Georgia, especially the Milledgeville State Mental Institution, about 30 miles away from Eatonton, as a principal setting in re-institutionalizing white supremacy after slavery. Using non-traditional references, such as personal letters, Haley cogently describes how Jim Crow was institutionalized through the imprisonment, torture and exploitation of black women. Haley explains, "As Georgia developed from an agricultural, plantation based economy to an industrial one, gendered racial terror fortified white patriarchal control over economic, political and social relations, thereby enshrining Jim Crow modernity."[29] Although Haley's social historical analysis occurs more than 30 years after Walker's characterization, we can rightly assume that Walker's Sophia was imprisoned in Milledgeville State Prison to which Haley refers.

Interestingly, FVSU's founding as an industrial school in 1895 followed on the proverbial heels of the time that these practices flourished. In *Ambiguous Lives: Free Women of Color in Rural Georgia* (1991), Adele Logan Alexander details antecedents of a discouraging and violent environment towards black women in post-slavery Georgia as a part of her cultural narrative about the family of Henry A. Hunt, a founder and president of Fort Valley industrial school, for whom the university's library is named. In citing numerous instances of brutalization of black girls and women, in part, for "wanting greater control of their working conditions"[30] and refusing to work as house servants, Alexander explains, "not infrequently, white men in Middle Georgia abused and humiliated black women."[31] Due to

> resentments (that) ran high when whites were faced with the loss of servants on whom they had always depended to prepare their food and attend to their every need, employers established governmentally sanctioned contract systems to control most black workers – including domestics.[32]

Although FVSU is located as close to the heart of Jim Crow modernity as one could possibly get, a history of counterhegemonic performance remains obscure. Fort Valley State is traditionally regarded as an institution where blacks could study for a couple of years beyond high school to obtain an "intensely practical kind of an education" as a teacher or to work on a farm.[33] Lena Horne (whose Uncle Frank Horne was an FVSU English professor and also served as Dean of Students) remembered FVSU as an educational environment in which blacks practiced duplicitous identities for white trustees who occasionally visited the campus. Horne characterized FVSU as similar to the school Ralph Ellison portrayed in *Invisible Man* (1952). In Ellison's first novel which won the 1953 National Book Award for Fiction, Ellison depicts a black institution of higher learning, presumably based on Tuskegee Institute where Ellison attended college for about three years. Tuskegee is located some 120 miles west of FVSU in the neighboring state of Alabama. FVSU and Tuskegee share similar histories and missions, especially with regard to respective commitments to training students as better farmers.

In keeping with a broader trend of leadership at HBCUs, black feminist performance at FVSU occurs within a tradition of marginalization. There has never been a permanent black woman president at Fort Valley State University in the school's 120 year history, nor is there a course of study or regular program dedicated to black feminist contribution. As a reflection of a ten-year trend among all HBCUs which has seen a reduction in the number of black women presidents of HBCUs due to (arguably) premature dismissal or untimely death, HBCU researchers and critics have wondered aloud, "Where Have All the Black Women Presidents Gone?"[34] As is also the case with performing arts, black women in leadership positions at HBCUs do not enjoy the same levels of institutional support as men, which can be thought to be to the institutions' detriment.

Lynching drama set in black schools

Annie Nathan Meyer's *Black Souls* (1938) is set on the campus of a black school in the Black Belt, a Southern region of the United State known as such due to a high population of blacks, stretching from east Texas to Virginia, north to Memphis and south to Tallahassee. Although the play was produced in 1938, its dialogue references 1923 or '24 as the present year which reflects the year it was written. The play centers upon the Magnolia School's founder and principal, Andrew Morgan, his wife, Phyllis, and their two children. Additionally, Phyllis' brother, David, teaches poetry at the school after he returns from Paris where he fought in World War I. The school's faculty, staff and students are preparing to receive distinguished guests in a public relations and fundraising event prevalent among such black schools.[35] The school's music quartet is rehearsing spirituals, and teachers are busy readying the facilities. The event guest list includes the state governor as well as Senator Verne and his daughter Luella with whom Phyllis and David are previously familiar. Unbeknownst to Andrew, Senator Verne raped Phyllis when she was 16, taking advantage of his position as a white man who wouldn't face punishment for assaulting a young black girl. Verne generously donates to the school as a way of continuing to harass Phyllis. David and Luella, on the other hand, entered into a mutual love affair while they were both working in France. Like her father's inappropriate and persistent advances toward Phyllis, Luella continues to pursue David despite his protestations. She repeatedly disregards his warnings about the danger she faces in seeking a relationship with him while living in the American South. Whether out of lust or love, both

Senator Verne and Louella actively pursue contact with Phyllis and David respectively without a real regard for their safety or well-being.

Within the play's six scenes, Annie Nathan Meyer inserts herself into a race-based controversy to construct a version of an interracial narrative set on a black school campus using white and black performance traditions. Not unproblematically, Meyer implicates Southern racism that would both rape black women and lynch black men to deny them dignity and justice. Meyer's challenge to white supremacist performance, however, incorporates stereotypical images of blacks as minstrels and pickaninnies, etc., further perpetuating "inauthentic" images about black people, provoking "racial division surrounding the ability of white playwrights to create authentic black characters in convincing situations."[36] Meyer's lynching play, therefore, appropriates both black narratives, whether espoused by prominent black (male) thinkers such as Du Bois[37] and Washington or traditional white supremacist narratives through the inclusion of minstrel images and "the lynching story," begging the question, why would Meyer write a play about lynching if not to seek justice on behalf of its victims?

A more nuanced observation about the contradictions in Meyer's play notes Meyer's identity as a Jewish American, not as a white woman, explaining her appropriation of both blackness and white supremacist performance. Meyer uses both traditions to negotiate her own identity as a newly assimilated white woman as opposed to engaging in active anti-lynching activism. As discussed in Lori Harris-Kahan's *The White Negress* (2011), Meyer's strategy was commonly used by Jewish women writers "to fashion new models of pluralistic identity that called into question the black-white binary and unseated whiteness as a universal ideal."[38] Unlike Jewish men, Jewish women's "literary and cultural representations" of blacks bring "gender and sexuality to the forefront" to "stage multivalent and highly ambivalent encounters among Jewishness, blackness and whiteness."[39] In *Black Souls*, Meyer's production of "a multivalent and highly ambivalent encounter" occurs through her authorship and production of a lynching play, a performative act which belongs to "a special class of actions that are derived from and may be plotted within a grid of power relationships," emphasizing "liminality over legibility and change over fixity," effectively "placing interpretive emphasis on actions rather than commodifiable objects."[40] Meyer appropriates black women's performative identity as lynching playwrights, an act that mirrored other Jewish cultural producers who negotiated white identity through the images they created.

Meyer uses a black educational institution as a frame in which to depict black-white conflict although she does not necessarily represent either side in a flattering way. Meyer appropriates issues related to the education of blacks, especially the danger black educators faced from white lynchers when seeking to teach black students knowledge and skills that would cause them to seek a world beyond white owned cotton fields and kitchens. The characters Andrew, Ulysses and David variously refer to black educators having to hide their true intentions in establishing schools for blacks in the South lest they be accused of improving "Negro knowledge and efficiency,"[41] which would genuinely threaten white supremacy. Even further, even though Andrew "jokes" about soliciting donations using the quartet's beautiful singing early in the play, the principal later recounts a horrific incident in which he was seized by a mob who tied a noose around his neck and dragged him until he was unconscious. While lying atop a gasoline soaked pile of wood, Andrew was finally given a chance to talk them out of burning him alive. The principal persuades the lynchers to spare his life by promising to not teach "the darkies" "above their position" as better "farmers . . . carpenters . . . and neighbors"[42]. Andrew admits to succumbing to the white terrorism so convincingly that the lynchers immediately donated $300 to his school, the most money he'd ever raised before. In this way, minstrelsy and lynching are presented as two degrading ways black men must perform in order to secure the money they need to build black educational institutions. Throughout the play, Andrew seeks to make the best of such incidents, repeatedly expressing his willingness to sacrifice for a greater good for his people. Such references by these black male characters represent a need to disguise their real objectives echoing Paul Lawrence Dunbar's 1896's poem "We Wear the Mask":

> We wear the mask that grins and lies
> Its hides our cheeks and shades our eyes, --
> This debt we pay to human guile;
> With torn and bleeding hearts we smile
> And mouth with myriad subtleties
> Why should the world be overwise
> In counting all our tears and sighs?
> Nay, let them only see us, while
> We wear the mask

We smile, but O great Christ, our cries
To Thee from tortured souls arise.
We sing, but oh, the clay is vile
Beneath our feet, and long the mile;
But let the world dream otherwise;
We wear the mask

Meyer perpetuates black stereotypes while at the same time criti-
quing white performance traditions, especially rape and lynching or
"nigger hunting," as David once calls it, when negotiating a white
identity for herself as opposed to any attempt to perform anti-lynching activism. Meyer's lynching play evidences Harris-Kahan's thesis
that "early appropriations in early 20th century American culture
produce and shore up white identity while simultaneously trou-
bling that self-same whiteness." By "minstrelizing" black activist,
intellectual and artistic efforts to combat white supremacy, Meyer
employs her Jewish imagination to depict blacks in a negative way,
as minstrels, extending the image beyond the vaudeville stage to cast
black educators and students in such roles as well. Meyer's depiction of blacks in this (condescending) way can be understood as tied
to negotiation of her own gender role in which she sought to fashion "models of New Womanhood" that were "opposed to the cult
of Victorian domesticity."[43] Although Meyer conventionally married and gave birth to a daughter, she is best known as a principal
founder of Barnard College, a prominent educational institution for
women in New York. Meyer established the women's college in 1887
in response to Columbia University's opposition to coeducational
opportunity. In spite of her progressive goals with regard to women's
education, Meyer worked as an anti-suffragist and in 1918 joined the
Daughters of the American Revolution.

Meyer's advocacy for women's education did not overshadow
her ambitions as a writer. In addition to editing *Women's Work in
America*, she authored several books on women's issues as well as
other dramatic work. Additionally, Meyer befriended and financially
patronized African American folklorist and writer Zora Neale Hurston who even provided feedback for *Black Souls*. Meyer and Hurston's relationship is subject to criticism, however, due to Hurston's
letters to Meyer in which she refers to herself as "your little pickan-
ninny." Meyer's unequal relationship status with Hurston as well as
Meyer's belittling characterization of educated black people in *Black
Souls* reflects how "the ability of Jewish women to achieve bourgeois

New Womanhood remained dependent on racial hierarchies that were replicated in their portrayals of cross racial relations on stage and in film."[44]

Staging "comm-university" productions at Fort Valley State University

One month before staging "Saving White Face" for the first time, the Joseph Adkins Players student drama group collaborated to co-produce a community and university, or "comm-university," performance of Regina Taylor's *Crowns: A Gospel Musical Play*. Such productions are traditional to Southern communities in which HBCUs are located, although Glenda Gill reports that early productions of black authored plays were not necessarily included in the repertoire.[45] Although an archive is incomplete, Fort Valley's community members sketch an oral history of "comm-university" productions in which the community collaborated with the drama club to produce shows under Adkins' direction. Drawing on the human and material resources of the local community in addition to a student organization budget, FVSU's black community theatre tradition reflects "the motive to connect" as "a driving force."[46] According to Margaret Wilkerson in her 1979 article "Redefining Black Theatre," black community theatre at FVSU is made distinct by "its attention to its audience."[47] By definition, FVSU comm-university theatre constitutes an "event – a dramatic occasion in which the true meaning of the theatre experience resides in what the audience takes away," allowing these collaborative productions "to treat theater as a laboratory of human interaction and potential rather than a museum piece. Above all else, Wilkerson observes, the "final psychic and spiritual health or condition of the audience"[48] takes precedence; therefore all production choices focus on facilitating the audience's experience. Staging Regina Taylor's *Crowns* in Fort Valley accomplished all of these objectives by "going back in time" to foreground Southern black history and celebrate folk culture and religious practice.

Crowns depicts a coming of age story of a teenaged black girl, Yolanda, who after losing her brother to gun violence, is sent from Brooklyn, New York, to live "down South" with her grandmother in Darlington, South Carolina. Yolanda's move represents a "reverse migration" pattern, moving in the opposite direction of the Great Migration, a period between 1910 and the 1960s when over

6 million blacks relocated from the South to the Northeast, Midwest and West to escape white terrorism and oppression, in search of economic, social and political opportunities. In fact, through Yolanda's move, Taylor documents a "Second Great Migration" trend in which blacks, somewhat disillusioned by hardships they continued to face in the North, returned to the South after the mid-1960s.[49] Most importantly, Yolanda's sojourn to the South marks the beginning of her rite of passage into womanhood as initiated by her grandmother and a community of women culture bearers. These women are marked as keepers of the culture through their practices of adornment, especially through wearing hats, or "crowns," to church on Sunday.

Not only does *Crowns* mark time through Yolanda's journey into adulthood but also through her return to "folk time," bygone eras of slavery, pre-slavery Africa as well as more modern eras recalled by her mentors. She also enters a realm in which time is slowed down thus facilitating lessons she must learn through the community of women's stories about hats. Due to her upbringing in the North where modern technology is thought to make time move faster, adjusting to a temporal difference between her old and new homes constitutes a major challenge which she must overcome. In her opening rap, Yolanda asserts, "BROOKLYN NEW YORK THAT'S WHERE I BELONG YOU CAN BE AN INDIVIDUAL THERE DO WANT YOU WANT AND NOBODY CARE," highlighting her pride in her Northern attitude in which her individuality is preferred over community. However, Yolanda's brother, who she is undoubtedly mourning, is thought to be a casualty of New York's "fast life," a reversal of the threat of white supremacist lynching in the pastoral South. Blacks left the South to escape certain types of white terrorism only to find "new," modern threats to their economic, social and physical well-being to which Yolanda's brother fell victim. Such paradoxical challenges were first explored by New Negro era intellectuals and artists who engaged in debates over "folk" versus modern culture in constructing images of blacks. Taylor reconsiders these themes through Yolanda who returns to the South, in part, to escape the modern dangers associated with a fast life and to learn to live as part of a community.

The impetus for staging *Crowns* derived from two distinguished members of the Fort Valley community who approached the JAP drama club about producing the play. Within days of one another, I was approached by both the wife of the tenth president, Mrs. Betty

Rivers, who is also a Fort Valley State College alumna; and Karan Kendrick, a native of Fort Valley and now a professional actress who grew up performing in plays directed by Joseph Adkins, participating in summer camps as well as producing shows herself. Ms. Kendrick's desire to stage *Crowns* was only exceeded by her expertise in staging the show since she was one of its very early touring company members.[50] Both Mrs. River's and Ms. Kendrick's respective choice of *Crowns* as a comm-university play reflected their understanding of the audience's connection to the show's "production material, physical location, and aesthetics."

My own production goal in co-staging *Crowns* echoed that of Mrs. Rivers and Ms. Kendrick in seeking to produce a show with which the Fort Valley audience could closely identify especially regarding its folklore and communication patterns. Since the play was set in a neighboring state, South Carolina, many of the cultural practices upon which *Crowns* is based, especially the ring shout and the tradition of black church women's adornment through wearing elaborate hats to church, were actively practiced by Fort Valley, Georgia, residents. These performance practices (as well as others) represented in *Crowns* functioned affectively between the university students, faculty, staff as well as audience members from the Fort Valley community, resulting in the filled to capacity crowd each night *Crowns* was performed. Even further, a live music ensemble made up of student musicians as well as local professionals played traditional gospel songs, helping to evoke a call and response participation between the actors and audience. Staging *Crowns* in Fort Valley facilitated a self-seeing, laying the groundwork for the town's political, social and economic transformation.[51]

Fort Valley State University's lynching play series 2012–2019

While in rehearsals for *Crowns*, George Zimmerman killed Trayvon Martin. Through class discussions held in three sections of communication courses I taught, I determined there to be a need to expose FVSU students to lynching plays as a grassroots, performance-based anti-lynching movement serving as a precursor to other such activism with which students might have been more familiar such as the Montgomery Bus Boycott and the March on Washington. Unbeknownst to us at the time, we were also studying lynching plays as a forerunner to #blacklivesmatter, #NeverAgainMSD and other hashtag social justice movements founded in response to senseless murders of young Americans.

Unlike *Crowns*, "Saving White Face" could not be cast using African American residents of Fort Valley nor FVSU's majority black student population. Staging "Saving White Face" required cast members from the other side of Fort Valley's proverbial tracks, its white residents. For this "comm-university" production, I reached out to Monica Nix, a Peach County High School drama instructor. Mrs. Nix, a 35-year teaching veteran, not only helped me cast the show from among her students, she even performed in the show as Louetta Cox, the play's minor character antagonist. Amanda Allen, an FVSU student, played as Ida, "Saving White Face's" principal narrator-character, the only African American. Ida performs as "Saving White Face's" narrator; however, she also doubles as two while male patriarchs at which moments she dons a white (Lone Ranger style) half mask. According to Wilkerson, such casting and prop choices force "the audience to challenge its assumptions and allows it to explore the mask of color as well as the humanity which lies beneath that mask."[52] "Saving White Face" effectively facilitated a forum in which both FVSU and Peach County High School students could address lynching performance as a critical, contemporary social and political issue.

Like *Crowns*, "Saving White Face's" 2012 staging also functioned as a "comm-university" performance, this time integrating Fort Valley's black and white community members to perform together on FVSU's campus as part of a dramatic arts curriculum. Although *Crowns* and "Saving White Face" may at first seem widely divergent as comm-university productions, staging both shows in one semester is actually definitive of black theatre, since *Crowns* helped Fort Valley residents and students see themselves including their "hopes, dreams, values systems and cultural patterns,"[53] fulfilling affective needs. Conversely, in staging "Saving White Face," the Joseph Adkins Players effectively addresses the unconventional needs of the audience, especially with regard to addressing issues of civil rights and social justice in a small Southern town. "Saving White Face" clarified lynching performances, revealing to students the structure of whiteness performance despite obfuscation by the lynching story and closely related (emergent) narrative traditionally used to cover up the acts. Through both shows, JAP approached performance events as forms of stimuli thereby treating "the theatre as a laboratory of human interaction and potential rather than a museum piece"[54] centered upon the Fort Valley comm-university.

Also, woven into the 2012 performance of "Saving White Face" were two original classical compositions written by my department colleague, Dr. Franklin Gross. Dr. Gross and I decided to weave the two works together due to similar themes. Three music students, robed in white, performed "Poem for Emmett Till" shortly after the murder was committed. As such, the musicians functioned like a Greek chorus who echoed the play's text and mood:

Poem for Emmett Till

Sleep Well, Emmett Till
Dream Big, Emmett Till
Live On, Emmett Till

Finally, upon the play's conclusion, a male student soloist performed Gross' operatic composition, "Live and Be Strong." The song's triumphant lyrics contrasted with the somber mood of the play's ending; however, the baritone vocals echoed a dramatic ending.

Live and Be Strong

There's no man can take my freedom
There's no freedom gone away
For to glory I am running
Running far to Heaven's gates
To Live and Be Strong
You can gain the loving freedom
Only love and freedom bring
You can walk the streets of Heaven
Where all tears are washed away
To Live and Be Strong

Depicting a Southern, segregated social environment, the set of "Saving White Face 2012" was made up of a kitchen table and chairs on the "domestic" side and a desk and typewriter in the "office." Props such as a shotgun, a typewriter and rotary telephone were used to help create the play's time and place. The stage lighting was limited; highlighting the stage's various realms but did not vary at all due to partially functioning equipment. The production incorporated several music recordings (including "Let the Good Times Roll" by Louis Jordan and "I Fall to Pieces" by Patsy Cline) that contributed to the play's blues aesthetic as well as the classical pieces previously mentioned.

Costuming consisted of cotton house dresses for the two white female characters, while Floyd was outfitted in a cotton lumberjack's shirt and khaki style work pants. Floyd's costuming can be thought to reflect a whiteness performance practice in which those seeking "security through identity" role play by wearing "survival gear" although such clothing is not necessary when living in modern society.[55] Clayton Pinochet wore modified business attire made up of black dress slacks and a white collared shirt that was rolled up to his elbow to indicate the Southern heat and humidity. Ida was costumed in a tuxedo style shirt, black pants and comfortable shoes. Her clothing was non-gender specific to mark her non-normative performance practices as well as facilitate easier transformation between narrator and character. Although the lynching occurred offstage, shotgun blast sound effects were used to connote the moment when the mob murders the young boy.

Your Blues Ain't Like Mine: a drama suite for social justice

Subsequent to our first production of "Saving White Face," the Joseph Adkins Players (JAP) re-staged the play as part of a two-play "anti-lynching drama suite." On March 3–5, 2014, the drama group presented *Your Blues Ain't Like Mine: A Drama Suite for Social Justice*,[56] responding to the recent shooting deaths of Reneisha McBride, Jonathan Ferrell and Jordan Davis. With a production goal of presenting a lynching play set in a white household as well as a black household, JAP staged both "Saving White Face" and Georgia Douglas Johnson's *Safe* (c.1929). Producing *Safe* at Fort Valley State University is also a noteworthy occasion since the drama depicts the 1899 lynching of Sam Hose (nee Holt), a native of nearby Marshallville, Georgia, which is only 10 miles from FVSU's campus. In fact, Fort Valley figures prominently in Hose's lynching since it was one of the towns in which "blacks were arrested on the possibility that they were the fugitive Hose."[57] After a ten-day manhunt, Hose was captured on a plantation just outside of Marshallville and extradited through Fort Valley on the way to Coweta County where he would be indicted for the murder of his former employer. Upon the stop in Fort Valley, his capturers (bounty hunters) commissioned a local black doctor to paint his

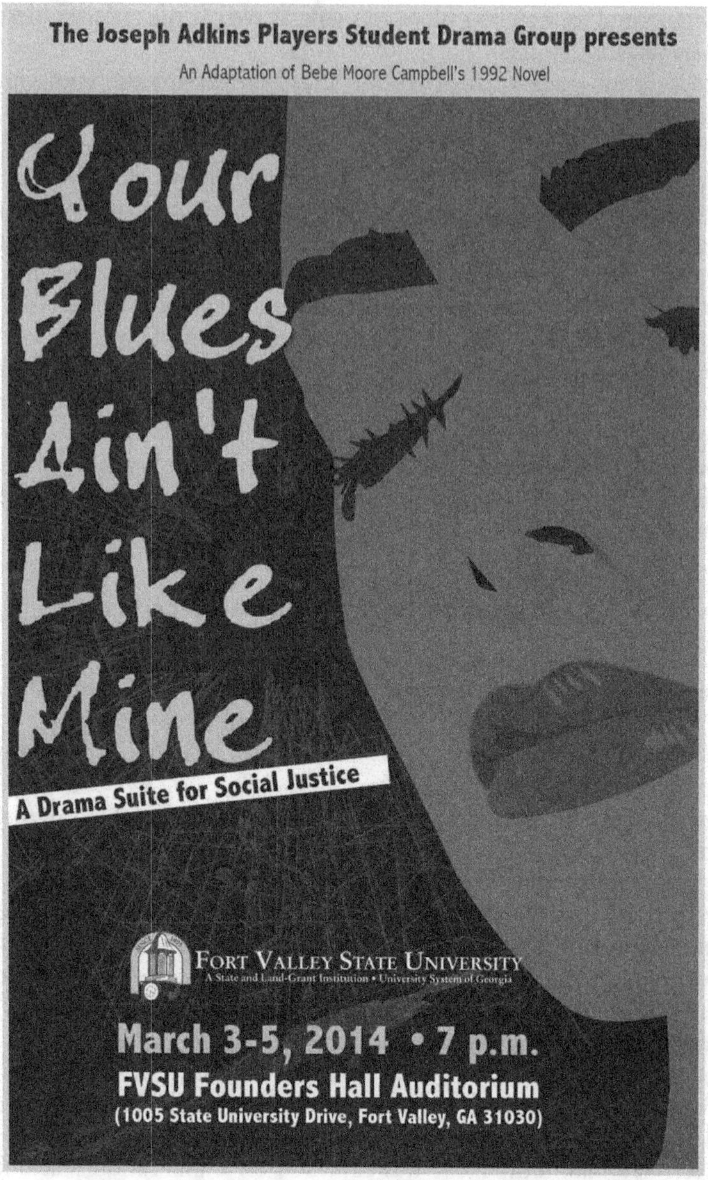

Figure 3.1 Playbill for Fort Valley State University's Joseph Adkins Players student drama group's March 3–5, 2014, production of Georgia Douglas Johnson's *Safe* (c. 1929) and "Saving White Face," a Chamber Theatre adaptation of Bebe Moore Campbell's novel, *Your Blues Ain't Like Mine* (1992).

face with burnt cork in order to disguise him so he wouldn't be easily recognized as they transported him.

Even further, the principal characters of the play, Liza and John
Pettigrew, have the same surname as C.W. Pettigrew for whom the
university's conference center is named. However, a connection
between the Pettigrew family and Georgia Douglass Johnson is yet
to be clearly established.

Johnson's use of the Pettigrew name may yet be explained but
her reason for dramatizing the lynching of Sam Hose is not hard
to understand. Hose's 1899 lynching is easily identifiable as one of
the most heinous American lynchings ever committed, especially
remarkable because of the way "the lynching cycle" played out,
including performance practices contained within it. As whiteness
cultural performance, Hose's lynching stands out as one of the earliest
modern versions of spectacle lynching since through it, newspapers,
railroad trains and distribution of body parts as souvenirs became
institutionalized within the lynching cycle's three classes of "preliminary, embedded and subsequent" performances.[58] Of the new ways
"the lynching story" was disseminated, Hale observes, "local and
regional newspapers took over the publicity, promotion and sale of
the event and began the development of a standardized, sensational-
ized narrative pattern that would dominate reporting of spectacle
lynchings through the 1940s."[59] Preliminary performances such as
an extended (ten-day) manhunt as well as the newspaper's narrative
and illustrated depiction of the white wife of the man whom Hose
was alleged to have raped but left alive ratcheted up a record setting
sized mob's level of frenzy. An embedded performance within Hose's
lynching included a burnt cork masking in which Hose was forced
to darken his face as a way of disguising him as bounty hunters extradited him to Atlanta. Hale and Arnold tie Hose's defacement to the
whiteness performance tradition of blackface minstrelsy which each
historian respectively interprets as a way of putting Hose in his place
as a "happy darky" or a way of projecting him into a subject position as a fool/clown. Sam Hose's spectacle lynching represents segue
from an era of blackface minstrelsy (1830–1930) to the lynching era
(1880–1930).

Hose's burnt cork performance contrasts with "burnt cork crimes"
as committed by white criminals who, as preliminary lynching performance, "darkened his or her face to evade detection and throw
suspicion across the racial divide."[60] Such crimes were so common
as to have been "regularly reported in newspapers and picked up

by anti-lynching activists" such as Frederick Douglass, Ida B. Wells-Barnett and the innocent black community members who were subjected to mob violence. Whether performed by white criminals or black lynching minstrels such as Sam Hose, both variations of burnt cork performance involved "consistent alteration of the performer's body. This body had an applied black face created from burnt cork mixed with grease; it was black without shading and usually darkened to an artificial extreme."[61] Whether altering the white or black body with burnt cork masking, only a desecration of black bodies resulted.

Although blackface minstrelsy is not often considered as an embedded performance within lynching, both whiteness performance practices were soon incorporated into another modern whiteness spectacle, D.W. Griffith's 1915 film *Birth of a Nation*, produced some 16 years after Hose's lynching. *Birth of a Nation*, which is widely regarded as a principal means of institutionalizing "the lynching story" through modern technology, incorporated burnt cork masking as well as a version of the narrative. Temporal boundaries as well as "performance behaviors" within each of these respective whiteness performance practices are understood to overlap and, like the three phases of Kirk Fuoss' "lynching cycle," function "as a wheel that keeps turning over, with one" whiteness performance practice "potentially serving as preliminary performances for another."

Finally, a "trophy gathering" of Hose's dismembered body parts, a subsequent lynching performance, functioned affectively among white lynchers who sold "pieces of bone" or "crisply cooked liver," displayed as contraband or collected as keepsakes. Harvey Young theorizes the clamoring for black body parts as lynching "souvenir, fetish and remain," existing "as both a metonym, referencing the lynching campaign, and as a synecdoche, reminding the viewer of the formerly whole body of which it is a part."[62] In other words, not only did Hose's body parts remind lynchers of the lynching event, the body parts actually "reactivate the expired performance event" thereby exceeding a cultural memory, but actually standing in as the event itself.

Georgia Douglas Johnson's *Safe* is an oft cited lynching play[63] by the most prolific black feminist playwright in the anti-lynching play genre. Johnson (1877?–1966), a native of Atlanta who relocated to Washington, D.C., to become a leader in the African American arts and culture community, was a multidisciplinary Harlem Renaissance era writer who composed "poems, plays, short stories and music."[64]

Johnson's cultural production, as well as her high output, reflects her intersectional approach to challenging white supremacist performance. Judith L. Stephens foregrounds Johnson's dramatic work in *The Plays of Georgia Douglas: From New Negro Renaissance to the Civil Rights Movement* (2006), a compiled collection and overview of 12 of her plays. In the monograph's introduction, Stephens discusses how Johnson's literary contribution is prolific not only due to her written work but must also include her black feminist leadership as convener of "the S Street Salon," a gathering of black artists, writers and teachers who would develop and share their work together. Stephens observes: "Studies of the New Negro Renaissance have overlooked the importance of Johnson's influence, possibly because she practiced an informal brand of community building that was closely tied to her home as a site of artistic activity."[65] If Johnson had been duly recognized as an innovator of modern theatre who, as an early performance studies artist-artivist, practiced theatre in a non-traditional space (her home), cultural scholars might have given her credit as a producer, creative director or dramaturg. Notable figures who frequented Johnson's Saturday night salon events included playwrights such as,

> Angelina Weld Grimke (*Rachel*, 1916), Willis Richardson (*The Chip Woman's Fortune*, 1923), Mary P. Burrill (*Aftermath*, 1919, and *They That Sit in Darkness*, 1919), Alice Dunbar Nelson (*Mine Eyes Have Seen*, 1918), May Miller (*Graven Images*, 1929), Zora Neale Hurston (*Color Struck*, 1925) and Marita Bonner (*The Purple Flower*, 1928).[66]

Stephens also notes African American cultural theorists Alain Locke's and W.E.B. Du Bois' respective attendance. Even further, Johnson's home incubated many dynamic collaborations, including that of Langston Hughes and Bruce Nugent who first conceived of *Fire!* (1926), a "provocative and experimental . . . journal of art and literature devoted to younger Negro artists."[67] In addition to African American artists, Johnson also welcomed white artists and formerly incarcerated men to her art house community.

Safe, one of Johnson's early lynching plays, depicts a black household who as husband, wife and mother-in-law, are busy preparing for the birth of their first child in 1893. John, Liza and Mandy begin to discuss the capture and jailing of "Sam Hosea," a 17-year-old young man who they know as the sole provider for his churchgoing single mother. Hosea was arrested for striking his "white boss" in retaliation as the two men disputed about wages. Soon, a trusted neighbor, Hannah, stops by the Pettigrew household to update the family about a mob that is assembling downtown with plans to kidnap Hosea from his jail cell with the intention of administering extralegal punishment, a lynching. Upon considering the heinous outcome of the situation, Liza becomes increasingly despondent, pondering, "What's little Nigger boys born for anyhow? I *sho* hopes mine will be a girl. – No, I don't want no boy baby to be hounded down and kicked round – No, I don't ever want to have no boy chile!" Mandy, Liza's mother, and Hannah try, in vain, to comfort Liza who grows more and more agitated. Mandy soon sends Hannah to get the doctor due to Liza's hysterical emotional state. The doctor arrives to deliver the baby who is born a healthy male. However, the doctor emerges from the birthing room to report that the baby boy is dead since Liza, upon learning his gender, strangles him to death. The play ends with both Mandy and John, as well as the audience, in a state of shock over how quickly a "blessing" of childbirth could turn tragic.

Non-normative motherhood in *Safe*

Johnson's play effectively foregrounds Liza's non-normative performance of womanhood and motherhood. First, Johnson presents Liza as a young woman who thinks critically about the ways her rights and those of black people are abused and exploited. Even while in the throes of labor, Liza quickly concludes that her newborn son is better off dead than subject to exploitation and victimization at the hands of white oppressors. Liza asks several questions about the progression of the lynching including questions that interrogate American democracy and justice. When Liza asks her husband, "You don't reckon they'll take Sam out of jail, do you John?" she poses a question inferring how lynchers kidnapped victims out of jail where they awaited trial, thereby denying the victims due process, a right guaranteed by the United States Constitution. Liza also poses a question about whether lynchers will unlawfully enter the Pettigrew home as the mob passes by the home in which the women listen and hide. Fearfully, "in awed tones," Liza asks her mother, "They wouldn't come in here would they, would they?" to which her mother responds by verbally consoling her while at the same time turning down the lights so as not to drawn attention to them. Here, through Mandy's contradiction in word and deed, Georgia Douglas Johnson theorizes the precarious position of the women whom the lawless mob would not necessarily refrain breaking in on, torturing (including rape) and murdering even though they are women who, according to dominant Victorian values espoused by whiteness narratives (i.e. "the lynching story"), are entitled to protection and even though Liza is pregnant. Johnson uses *Signifying*, which is both a black "verbal dueling" tactic as well as "a way of encoding messages or meanings which involves, in most cases, an element of indirection"[68] to indicate black women and children's "precarity" or "politically induced condition in which certain populations suffer from failing social and economic networks of support and become differentially exposed to injury violence and death."[69] When Mandy's actions acknowledge that neither the women's gender nor their position inside the house guarantee their well-being, Johnson depicts Mandy as *Signifying* on Liza's questions so as to both keep her daughter calm as well as do what little she can to protect them from the mob. Even though Mandy tells her daughter to focus on giving birth instead of worrying about the lynching happening outside their doorstep, exhorting Liza to "born him safe," Johnson *Signifies* on the concepts of womanhood and the protection supposedly afforded women since there is no guarantee of safety for black women, children or men even though the Constitution guarantees "life, liberty and the pursuit of happiness." As a thinking woman, Liza understands that her mother is *Signifying* on her birth process and decides to, in her own way, practice *Signifying* on motherhood.

Liza's expressed wish to have a girl instead of a boy reflects her understanding of a black boy's precarity in a white supremacist society. Not only does Liza understand a black boy's positionality intellectually, she acts upon her knowledge by strangling her newborn son. Liza's actions are actively contrasted with theological (presumably, Christian) values of accepting one's fate as "God's will" through the words of Liza's mother, Mandy Grimes, who tells Liza, "Hush, honey, that's a sin. God sends us what he wants us to have – we can't pick and choose." Despite her mother's admonition, Liza does make a choice. Liza chooses to interpret her mother's words in her own way, inferring her conclusion that God is a white man or her atheism. Liza goes on to choose the fate of her son, death, rather than subject him to "God's will." Not only does Liza's performance diverge from prevalent constructions of womanhood in which women practice faith in lieu of critical thought, but Liza also performs as a non-normative mother who gives life but also takes it away.

Liza's questions further call to mind the 1918 lynching of Mary Turner, a young married and pregnant mother of two who upon protesting the murder of her husband Hazel "Hayes" Turner was lynched herself. Even worse, Turner's baby was cut from her stomach and stomped to death. Symbolically, the wombs of black mothers are equated with black people's homes, neither of which is "safe from the lynchers." It should be noted here that through Georgia Douglas Johnson's use of the actual historical lynchings of both Sam Hose and Turner as the basis of *Safe*,[70] Johnson performs a "comparative symbology" in which she

> contextual(izes) symbols in the concrete, historical fields of their use by "(wo)men alive" as they act, react, transact and interact socially. Even when the symbolic is the *inverse* of the pragmatic reality, it remains intimately in touch with it, affects and is affected by it, provides the positive figure with its negative ground thereby delimiting each," and winning for "cosmos" a new territory.[71]

One way Johnson "wins" new territory is by writing into being a new (black) feminist subject, a non-normative mother.

A mother of the dead

When *Safe* opens, Liza is seated at a sewing machine creating "flannel belly bands" and night gowns in preparation for her newborn's birth. In this way, Johnson frames Liza as a traditional mother who prepares for childbirth in a manner reflecting Victorian era values. Motherhood is performed as an abstraction characterized by labor associated with grooming and dressing a child, preparing it to be seen but not necessarily heard. However, upon hearing the news of Sam Hose's lynching and then his actual cries for his mother, Liza abandons her sewing, becoming preoccupied with sounds of the whiteness performance as they reflect the lynching's progress. Liza first sympathizes with Hose's mother whom she knows as "a little skinny brown-skinned woman. Belong to our church. She use to bring Sam along pretty regular all the time." Quickly, Liza's idea of motherhood transforms into a realization of her inability to protect her own child, no matter how well she grooms him. As Sam's lynching progresses, Liza becomes increasingly anxious, triggering her to go into labor. Sam and Liza's unborn child respectively enter liminal phases of death and life. As Sam Hosea enters the lynching cycle through which he is tortured and eventually killed, Liza's child enters her birth canal through which it will soon be born. However, Johnson takes the black woman's childbirth one step beyond its natural process to depict the baby boy's birth as a rite of passage into a white supremacist society in which the child will likely be subject to the lynching cycle. In this way, Johnson positions Sam's lynching cycle as a symbolic equivalent of Liza's childbirth, albeit an "inverse of the pragmatic reality"[72] of Sam's death. Instead of being subject to a lynching cycle, a liminal stage during which all legal and constitutional rights are denied the black victim, Liza strangles her baby boy, inverting the norm of motherhood in which a child's mother seeks to protect it rather than kill it. Even worse as a black boy child, Liza sees subjugation is never-ending beginning at birth, proceeding to an arbitrary ending due to the white supremacist society into which it was born. Rather than exposing her child to such an ongoing ordeal, Liza kills her baby upon its birth to become a non-normative mother of the dead rather than a traditional mother whose child lives under such topsy-turvy circumstances.

In conclusion, Georgia Douglass Johnson's depiction of Liza as a non-normative mother in *Safe* marks lynching as symbolic ritual, a critical identification since "symbols . . . are crucially involved in structures of societal change"[73] through which American society has continuously undergone since the Reconstruction era. Since cultural symbols are "social and cultural dynamic systems, shedding and gathering meaning over time and altering in form," through anti-lynching drama, Johnson uses the lynching cycle to examine the birth of a black mother's (Liza's) baby as a "comparative symbology" practice to Sam Hose's death. Liza's birth process might also be understood as comparable to the film *Birth of a Nation* as a modern whiteness performance practice, especially since the film unethically functions as spectacle, as opposed to cultural performance. Furthermore, through lynching drama such as *Safe*, Johnson "plays with"[74] or makes use of the (dis)order of lynching performance to create new "models, symbols, paradigms, etc." of motherhood; in this case, creating a new non-normative subject, a black mother of the already dead who cannot be subject to a Jim Crow Era's emerging performances of exploitation, torture and murder.

Notes

1 "Saving White Face" (2012) was staged as a part of Fort Valley State University's second annual Research Day activities.

2   Fuoss, "Lynching Performances," 9–29.
3   George Zimmerman was acquitted of Trayvon Martin's murder on July 14, 2013. See www.nytimes.com/2013/07/14/us/george-zimmerman-verdict-tray-von-martin.html.
4   Harry Elam and David Krasner, *African American Performance and Theatre History: A Critical Reader* (New York, NY: Oxford University Press, 2001), 6.
5   Shari Dorantes Hatch, "A Herstory of the #BlackLivesMatterMovement," in *Encyclopedia of African American Writing* (Amenia, NY: Greyhouse Publishing, 2018). https://search-credoreference-com.proxygsu-for1.galileo.usg.edu/content/entry/ghaaw/a_herstory_of_the_blacklivesmatter_movement/0.
6   Mitchell, *Living With Lynching*, 10.
7   Ibid.
8   Lindsey, *Colored No More*.
9   "May Miller Papers," Emory University.
10 Randolph Edmonds, "The Negro Little Theatre Movement," *The Negro History Bulletin* 12 (January 1, 1949), 4.
11 Ibid, 83.
12 Ibid.
13 Ibid, 86.
14 Ibid.
15 Alain Locke and Montgomery Edwards (eds.), *Plays of a Negro Life: A Sourcebook of Native American Drama* (Westport, Conn: Negro Universities Press, 1970), 8.
16 Ibid.
17 Ibid, 92.
18 Edmonds, "The Negro Little Theatre Movement," 93.
19 Ibid.
20 Bernard L. Peterson, *The African American Theatre Directory 1816–1960: A Comprehensive Guide to Early Black Theater Organizations, Companies, Theaters and Performing Groups* (Westport, CT: Greenwood Publishing, 1997), 73-74.
21 Ibid, 55–56.
22 Ibid.
23 Ibid, 73-74.
24 Ronald Roach, "Black Theater in Transition," *Black Issues in Higher Education* 14, no. 12 (August 7, 1997), 07420277.
25 "Welcome to Fort Valley" www.fortvalleyga.org, https://fortvalleyga.org/.
26 See Donnie D. Bellamy, *Light in the Valley: A Pictoral History of Fort Valley State College since 1985* (Virginia Beach, VA: Donning Co. Publishing, c.1996).
27 Since her appearance in the movie *The Color Purple* (1984), Oprah Winfrey emerged as a leading media executive, philanthropist, television and film actress and talk show host.
28 Haley, *No Mercy Here*.
29 Ibid, 12.
30 Adele Logan Alexander, *Ambiguous Lives: Free Women of Color in Rural Georgia 1789–1879* (Fayetteville, AR: University of Arkansas Press, 1991).
31 Ibid, 149.
32 Ibid, 147.
33 Lena Horne, *Lena* (New York, NY: Doubleday, 1965), 29.

34 Crystal deGregory, "Where Have All the Black Women HBCU Presidents Gone?" *HBCUdigest.com*, November 28, 2016, https://hbcudigest.com/where-have-all-the-black-women-hbcu-presidents-gone/.

35 Such an event was referenced in Richard Wright's *Invisible Man* (1952) and was also executed at Fort Valley State University.

36 Perkins and Stephens, *Strange Fruit*, 134.

37 The title of the play *Black Souls* is a reference to W.E.B. Du Bois' treatise *The Souls of Black Folk* (1903).

38 Lori Harrison Kahan, *The Colored Negress: Literature, Minstrelsy and the Black-Jewish Imaginary* (Newark, NJ: Rutgers University Press, 2010), 10.

39 Ibid.

40 Blocker, *Where Is Ana Mendieta?* 24.

41 Perkins and Stephens, *Strange Fruit*, 147.

42 Ibid, 148.

43 Kahan, *The Colored Negress*, 11.

44 Ibid.

45 Glenda Gill, "The Transforming Power of Performing the Classics in Chocolate, 1949–1954, in What Is Black Play: Forum on Black Theatre?" *Theatre Journal: Black Performance* 7, no. 57 (December 2005), 592–96.

46 Margaret B. Wilkerson, "Redefining Black Theatre," *The Black Scholar* (July-August 1979), 38.

47 Ibid, 35.

48 Ibid, 34.

49 See Greg Toppo and Paul Overberg, "After Nearly 100 Years, Great Migration begins reversal," *www.usatoday.com, March 18, 2015*, www.usatoday.com/story/news/nation/2015/02/02/census-great-migration-reversal/21818127/.

50 Karan Kendrick performed in *Crowns* as "Jeanette" at the Goodman Theatre in 2004.

51 See David Krasner, "African American Performance in the Harlem Renaissance" in A Beautiful Pageant: African American Theatre, Drama and Performance in the Harlem Renaissance 1910–1927 (New York: Palgrave MacMillan, 2002), 1–14.

52 Staging *Crowns* in Fort Valley in March 2012 might be said to be indirectly tied to the November 13, 2013, election of Barbara Williams, the town's first black woman mayor. Mayor Williams is both a Fort Valley State alumnus as well as a retired professor.

53 Wilkerson, "Redefining Black Theatre," 36.

54 Ibid, 35.

55 Ibid.

56 Victor Papanek, *Design for the Real World: Human Ecology and Social Change* (Chicago, IL: Academy Chicago Publishers, 1984), 15–16.

57 In order to appeal to a broader market, this production was named for Bebe Moore Campbell's 1992 novel which was a New York Times bestseller.

58 Edwin T. Arnold, *What Virtue There Is in Fire: Cultural Memory and the Lynching of Sam Hose* (Athens, GA: University of Georgia Press, 2009), 80–81.

59 In "Lynching Performances," Fuoss explains an inexact demarcation of the lynching cycle as "preliminary performances occur between the alleged precipitating crime and the mob's seizure of its victim. Embedded performances occur after the mob's seizure of its victim and include all performances up to and including the extralegal public execution. Finally subsequent performances include all those that happen after the event."

60 Hale, *Making Whiteness*, 210.
61 Fuoss, "Lynching Performances," 10.
62 Stephen Johnson (ed.), *Burnt Cork: Traditions and Legacies of Blackface Minstrels* (Amherst, MA: University of Massachusetts Press, 2012), 7–8.
63 Harvey Young, "The Black Body as Souvenir in American Lynching" *Theatre Journal* 57 (2005), 656.
64 See Mitchell, *Living With Lynching* (2011); and Lindsey, *Colored No More* (2017).
65 Stephens, *The Plays of Georgia Douglas Johnson*, 1.
66 Ibid, 16.
67 Ibid, 14.
68 Ibid, 16.
69 Mitchell-Kernan, "Signifying," 311.
70 Judith Butler, "Performativity, Precarity and Social Politics," *AIBR: Revista de Antropología Iberoamericana* 4, Número 3 (Septiembre-Diciembre 2009), I-XIII. www.aibr.org. (Madrid: Antropólogos Iberoamericanos en Red. 25), VII.
71 It should be noted that Johnson's anti-lynching plays were noteworthy for their depictions of actual historical lynching performances as in *Safe*, as well as *And Yet They Paused* and *A Bill to Be Passed*, versus looser characterizations of the practice.
72 Turner, *From Ritual to Theatre*, 23.
73 Ibid.
74 Ibid, 22.
75 Ibid.

Bibliography

Alexander, Adele Logan. 1991. *Ambiguous Lives: Free Women of Color in Rural Georgia 1789–1879*. Fayetteville, AR: University of Arkansas Press.
Arnold, Edwin T. 2009. *What Virtue There Is in Fire: Cultural Memory and the Lynching of Sam Hose*. Athens, GA: University of Georgia Press.
Blocker, Jane. 1999. *Where Is Ana Mendieta: Identity, Performance and Exile*. Durham, NC: Duke University Press.
Butler, Judith. 2009. "Performativity, Precarity and Social Politics." *Revisita de Antropologia Iberoamericana*: 1–13.
Campbell, Bebe Moore. 1992. *Your Blues Ain't Like Mine*. New York, NY: One World Book.
Edmonds, Randolph. 1949. "The Little Negro Theatre Movement." *The Negro History Bulletin*: 82–94.
Elam, Harry, and David Krasner. 2001. *African American Performance and Theatre History*. New York, NY: Oxford University Press.
Fuoss, Kirk. 1999. "Lynching Performances, Theatres of Violence." *Text and Performance Quarterly*: 1–37.
Gill, Glenda. 2005. "The Transforming Power of Performing Classics in Chocolate, 1949–1954." *Theatre Journal* 7, no. 57: 592–96.
Hale, Elizabeth Grace. 1998. *Making Whiteness: The Culture of Segregation in the South 1890–1940*. New York, NY: Vintage Books.

Haley, Sarah. 2016. *No Mercy Here: Gender, Punishment and Making of Jim Crow Modernity*. Chapel Hill, NC: University of North Carolina Press.

Hatch, Shari Dorantes (ed.). 2018. "A Herstory of the #BlackLivesMatter Movement." *Encyclopedia of African American Writing*. Accessed May 21, 2019. https://search-credoreference-com.proxygsu-for1.galileo.usg.edu/content/entry/ghaaw/a_herstory_of_the_blacklivesmatter_movement/0.

Horne, Lena. 1965. *Lena*. New York, NY: Doubleday.

Johnson, Stephen (ed.). 2012. *Burnt Cork: Traditions and Legacies of Blackface Minstrels*. Amherst, MA: University of Massachusetts Press.

Kahan, Lori Harrison. 2010. *The Colored Negress: Literature, Minstrelsy and the Black-Jewish Imaginary*. Newark, NJ: Rutgers University Press.

Lindsey, Treva. 2017. *Colored No More: Reinventing Black Woman in Washington D.C.* Urbana-Champaign, IL: University of Illinois Press.

"May Miller Papers." 1909–1990. *Stuart A. Rose Manuscript*. Atlanta, GA: Archives and Rare Book Library, Emory University.

Mitchell, Koritha. 2011. *Living With Lynching: African American Lynching Plays, Performance and Citizenship, 1830–1930*. Urbana, IL: University of Illinois Press.

Mitchell-Kernan, Claudia. 1990. "Signifying." In *Mother Wit from the Laughing Barrel: Readings in the Interpretation of Afro-American Folklore*, edited by Alan Dundes, 310–28. Jackson, MS: University of Mississippi Press.

Papanek, Victor. 1984. *Design for the Real World: Human Ecology and Social Change*. Chicago, IL: Academy Chicago Publishers.

Perkins, Kathy A., and Judith L. Stephens. 1998. *Strange Fruit: Plays on Lynching by American Women*. Bloomington, IN: Indiana University Press.

Peterson, Bernard L. 1997. *The African American Theatre Directory 1816–1960: A Comprehensive Guide to Early Black Theatre Organizations, Companies, Theatres and Performing Groups*. Westport, CT: Greenwood Publishing.

Turner, Victor. 1982. *From Ritual to Theatre: The Human Seriousness of Play*. New York, NY: PAJ Publications.

Wilkerson, Margaret. 1979. "Redefining Black Theatre." *The Black Scholar*: 32–42.

Wright, Richard. 1952. *Invisible Man*. New York, NY: Random House.

Young, Harvey. 2005. "The Black Body as Souvenir in American Lynching." *Theatre Journal*: 639–57.

Epilogue – we call bullshit!

Emma Gonzalez, a senior at Marjorie Stoneman Douglas High School in Parkland, Florida, delivered an impassioned 11-minute speech on February 17, 2018, after surviving a school shooting three days prior that killed 17 of her classmates and left at least 17 others injured. With tears streaming down her face, Gonzalez spoke at a gun control rally at the Broward County courthouse, repeating the phrase "We call BS!" to refute fallacious arguments Stoneman Douglas students regularly encounter as residents of Florida where gun laws are considered permissive. Even further, gun control is an issue at the heart of several American mass school shootings which became increasingly more urgent as a matter of national health and safety since the 1999 Columbine High School shooting. Between 1999 and 2018, the span of Gonzalez's entire lifetime, at least 25 active school shootings occurred in America.

The image of Gonzalez speaking was remarkable for many reasons related to her content and speaking style. Gonzalez's shaved head marked her gender performance as non-normative and her light brown skin starkly inverted the white supremacist gun norms she fervently challenged. For those deeply familiar with black feminist performance practices like myself, I immediately recognized Gonzalez's performance as a re-play of Ida B. Wells-Barnett's aforementioned October 1892 address in which she "talked through tears" at a Brooklyn, New York, fundraising show in her honor. While speaking at a black clubwoman event of high production value, Wells-Barnett's tearful speech delivery in which she conveyed her emotion around losing three friends to lynching as well as her exile from Memphis proved effective in advancing her activism in the same way as Gonzalez's speechmaking did. Watching Gonzalez speak via live streaming on national news outlets as well as again and again on YouTube and again on a Smartboard projector in class with my communications students, called to mind Schechter's description of Wells-Barnett continuing to speak in a steady voice, despite a "streaming face." As in Wells-Barnett's case, the image of Gonzalez "talking through tears" was "rich with meaning" since "tears were much more acceptable for a (young) proper lady than anger or its cousin, sarcasm."[1] Gonzalez's speech, delivered more than 125 years later, effectively expressed her sadness, anger and sarcasm and can be considered forward movement in the realm of gender politics. However, the century old repetition of a black feminist blueswoman performance represented more of a changing same with regard to another generation "who are made crazy again and again, by dominant social formations that select against them."[2] The "lynching cycle" continues until the present; this time, the white supremacist performance takes the phallic form of assault rifles augmented to fire torturous bullets rapidly before a shooter can be apprehended or killed. Unlike early lynching performances in which lynchers faced no fear of accountability whether their identity was known to law enforcement officials or not, mass shooters are now able to inflict life shattering damage upon the lives of large numbers of people in spite of the likelihood that they *will* be captured or killed.

Lone white supremacist murderers seem to have upgraded their modern technology apparatus and substituted the lynch mob impulse for a mass destruction impulse. The weapons they use may have changed, but the message remains the same. As the title of Georgia Douglas Johnson's play foretold, there are no "safe" places in American society where its citizens are free, "free from the lynchers."

Less than five years earlier three black women, Alicia Garza, Patrisse Cullors and Opal Tometi, collaborated to launch a grassroots movement, #blacklivesmatter, spawned by the February 2012 murder of Trayvon Martin. In response to outrage expressed on social media, a hashtag campaign began which soon became a rallying cry for those protesting Martin's death and then the deaths of other innocent young blacks that followed over the next couple of years. From 2013–2014 Garza, Cullors and Tometi organized a movement that expanded to include more than 40 chapters. According to their website's "herstory" page, the organization identifies itself as follows:

> Black Lives Matter is an ideological and political intervention in a world where Black lives are systematically and intentionally targeted for demise. It is an affirmation of Black folks' humanity,

our contributions to this society, and our resilience in the face of deadly oppression.[3]

Garza, Cullors and Tometi's collaboration brings to mind the anti-lynching drama movement in which black feminist playwrights worked collectively to protest lynching performances through a genre of American dramatic art. In fact, #blacklivesmatter functions as a repetition of the earlier movement, four or five generations removed. In this latest iteration, black feminist activists are known for their inclusive community values, vowing not to make the same mistakes of movements past that excluded or marginalized non-normative performances of race, gender and class. Such self-reflexivity demonstrates a noteworthy commitment to honor black lives without reference to a politics of respectability that long buried Ida B. Wells-Barnett's anti-lynching activism, Anna Julia Cooper's black feminist cultural criticism, Angelina Weld Grimke's poems, short stories and anti-lynching plays as well as the anti-lynching play genre in its entirety. #Blacklivesmatter continues the work of these earlier black feminist performance-based movements which sought to invert a social, political and economic order that subverts American justice by upending a rule of law.

The Legacy Museum and the National Memorial for Peace and Justice opened on April 26, 2018, in Montgomery, Alabama, to commemorate the lynching of 4,400 victims between 1887 and 1950.[4] The museum garners national attention kicked off with a celebrity driven ribbon cutting ceremony. Through a combination of visual art, cutting edge technology and exhibitions, the museum and memorial mark Montgomery, Alabama, as a historical site where slavery and Jim Crow segregation and lynching flourished.

In *Preaching the Blues*, a black feminist performance trope of anti-lynching drama is repeated as cross generational activism protesting against emergent lynching performance. Blueswoman performance refutes the white supremacist performance complex that, as "a protracted form of terrorism,"[5] continues to traumatize black people across generations and for which there has been no comprehensive redress. Consequently, black feminist anti-lynching performances, including anti-lynching drama, must be repeated to provide clarification and purification in the moment; yet, they are unable to prevent re-injury by those white supremacist lynching performers who refuse to break the lynching cycle.

Notes

1 Schechter, *Ida B. Wells-Barnett and American Reform*, 20.
2 English, *Unnatural Selections*, 121.
3 Hatch, "A Herstory of the #BlackLivesMatterMovement." https://search-credoreference-com.proxygsu-for1.galileo.usg.edu/content/entry/ghaaw/a_herstory_of_the_blacklivesmatter_movement/0.
4 "The National Memorial for Peace and Justice," *Legacy Museum and National Memorial for Peace and Justice*. Accessed May 23, 2019. https://museumandmemorial.eji.org/memorial.
5 English, *Unnatural Selections*, 127.

Index

Printed in the United States
by Baker & Taylor Publisher Services